Hymns for the People

WORDS EDITION

Edited by
David Peacock

with

Roger Mayor, Christopher Norton
and
Michael Perry (Words Editor)

Marshall Pickering
An Imprint of HarperCollinsPublishers

JUBILATE 2000
Jubilate 2000 is an imprint of Jubilate Hymns

Marshall Pickering is an imprint of
HarperCollins*Religious*
Part of HarperCollins*Publishers*
77–85 Fulham Palace Road,
Hammersmith, London W6 8JB

This edition first published in Great Britain in 1993 by Marshall Pickering

Reprinted: 95 94 93
Impression number: 10 9 8 7 6 5 4 3 2 1

The compilers assert the moral right to be identified as the compilers of this work

ISBN 0 551 02511 5

Music edition ISBN 0 551 02510 7

Typeset by Barnes Music Engraving Ltd, East Sussex, England
Printed and bound in Great Britain by Scotprint Ltd, Musselburgh, Edinburgh

A catalogue record for this book is available from the British Library

Also edited by the Jubilate group:

Hymns for Today's Church
Church Family Worship
Carols for Today
Carol Praise*
Play Carol Praise*
Let's Praise!*
Come Rejoice!*
The Wedding Book*
Lollipops for organ*
The Dramatised Bible*
Prayers for the People*
Psalms for Today
Songs from the Psalms
World Praise*

* *Available from HarperCollins*

Preface

Why another hymn book?
Recent years have seen in some churches a radical reduction in the number of 'hymns' within their worship repertoire. Many established texts have been in the danger of being lost to numerous worshipping communities.

There are several reasons for this. Firstly, the musical style that has accompanied hymn-texts in the past is out of keeping with the prevailing musical vocabulary of some congregations. The organ is very rarely used, if at all, and the music group is the main accompaniment. The majority of the congregation has an affinity with a more contemporary style. Secondly, the hymn texts that are used offer outmoded phrases and expressions. Established hymns have been regarded by some as being out of step with the current textual vocabulary of the rest of the church's worshipping language.

The value of hymns
For the purposes of this book, we have defined a hymn as a text that develops a theme in logical sequence. We have deliberately avoided defining a hymn by its musical characteristics. We believe that, as such, hymns are an essential part of our worship diet because of their intrinsic nourishment value. They are complimentary to worship songs. *Hymns for the People* is an attempt to make hymns more accessible to churches who have largely dispensed with them.

The words
The careful revision of texts has been the product of many years of research by Jubilate editorial teams. Accordingly, a group of writers within Jubilate has ensured that the selection of texts for *Hymns for the People* is both relevant and appropriate to contemporary worship. We have also tried to include a number of texts produced by hymn writers within the last ten years. We have attempted to provide items that cover a breadth of themes and a range of uses within community worship. However, it should be noted that some of the credal hymns do not completely represent the creed on which they are based. Some of the hymns include indications for dividing the congregation into two groups to sing either particular verses or sections of the hymn. We have avoided using *men* and *women*, since this may be inappropriate in some congregations.

The music
The music for *Hymns for the People* gives the book its own unique contribution. Every hymn-tune has been extensively re-arranged for music-group. Details of the musical arrangements are given in the preface to the Music Edition. Some of the recent texts have been given new settings in the style of current worship songs. There are also a number of traditional texts with new settings. We believe it is now possible to use established hymns creatively within flows of praise and worship; for songs and hymns to be used alongside each other with stylistic credibility.

Finding your way around
The hymns are arranged alphabetically, but an extensive thematic index at the back of the Music Edition together with a biblical index covering three thousand references provide an invaluable help to the worship planner. The musician will find both metrical and alphabetical indexes to the tunes included in the Music Edition. A selection of scripture-based prayers suitable for community worship are found at the end of the Words Edition.

Hymns for the People is an attempt to rescue hymn-texts from being put on the shelf. We hope that church communities who have genuinely found it difficult to incorporate many hymns within their worship will now be able to broaden their repertoire and that congregations will be enabled to use material that provides in-depth vocabulary for praise, thanksgiving, heart worship and response to God in both lifestyle and service.

A full set of acknowledgements appears below, but I would especially like to thank Michael Perry, whose original vision it was to produce such a book, and Roger Mayor and Christopher Norton for their talented and stimulating assistance. Together, we dedicate this hymnbook to the service of worshipping communities and to the glory of God.

David Peacock (Editor)

Legal Information and Acknowledgements

Reprinting
Those seeking to reprint material in this book which is the property of Jubilate Hymns or associated authors and composers (attributed '/Jubilate Hymns') may write to the Copyright Manager, Jubilate Hymns Ltd, 61 Chessel Avenue, Southampton SO2 4DY. In the United States of America these copyrights and those of Timothy Dudley-Smith are administered by Hope Publishing Company, Carol Stream, Illinois 60188.

Items by authors and composers administered by Jubilate, together with those held by some major copyright holders (Thankyou Music, CopyCare, Make Way Music etc.) are covered by the licence scheme operated by the Christian Copyright Licensing Ltd, 26 Gildredge Road, Eastbourne, East Sussex BN21 4SA (0323 417711).

Recording and Broadcasting
Jubilate Hymns and associated authors and composers, and Word & Music are members of the Mechanical Copyright Protection and Performing Right Societies.

Acknowledgements
We are grateful to all those who contributed to the compilation of *Hymns for the People*. We owe our thanks most particularly to those authors and composers who readily created or adapted their work to meet the needs of the book. We mention especially Roger Mayor and Christopher Norton for their expertise, help and support; Christopher Idle, Michael Saward, Jane Sinclair and Geoff Twigg for their help with the texts; Angela Griffiths, Clifford Roseweir, Jane Peacock, Valerie Parker and Ann Jenner for getting the material ready for publication.

For the major task of copyright clearance and assistance in preparing the work we are deeply grateful to Bunty Grundy of Jubilate Hymns.

David Peacock (Editor)
Michael Perry (Words Editor)

1

From Isaiah 9
© Pearl Beasley / Jubilate Hymns

1 A child is born for us today,
  a son to us is given;
  the saviour comes to guide our way
  and lead us up to heaven.
    They'll call him 'Wonderful',
    heavenly 'Counsellor'.
  We'll call him 'Jesus.'

2 He comes to be the 'Prince of peace',
  to all the world a friend;
  his mighty love will never cease,
  his kingdom will not end.
    They'll call him 'Mighty God',
    'Eternal Father'.
  We'll call him 'Jesus'.

3 On those who walk the darkest way
  has dawned a shining light
  far brighter than the brightest day,
  a great and glorious sight.
    O come, Emmanuel,
    our God, be with us!
  O come, Lord Jesus!

2

© Timothy Dudley-Smith

1 A purple robe, a crown of thorn,
  a reed in his right hand;
  before the soldiers' spite and scorn
  I see my saviour stand.

2 He bears between the Roman guard
  the weight of all our woe;
  a stumbling figure bowed and scarred
  I see my saviour go.

3 Fast to the cross's spreading span,
  high in the sunlit air,
  all the unnumbered sins of man
  I see my saviour bear.

4 He hangs, by whom the world was made,
  beneath the darkened sky;
  the everlasting ransom paid,
  I see my saviour die.

5 He shares on high his Father's throne,
  who once in mercy came;
  for all his love to sinners shown
  I sing my saviour's name.

3

Henry Francis Lyte

1 Abide with me, fast falls the eventide;
  the darkness deepens: Lord, with me abide.
  When other helpers fail and comforts flee,
  help of the helpless, O abide with me.

2 Swift to its close ebbs out life's little day;
  earth's joys grow dim, its glories pass away.
  Change and decay in all around I see –
  you never change, O Lord: abide with me!

3 I need your presence every passing hour:
  what but your grace
    can foil the tempter's power?
  Who like yourself
    my guide and strength can be?
  Through cloud and sunshine, Lord,
    abide with me!

4 I have no fear with you at hand to bless;
  ills have no weight and tears no bitterness.
  Where is death's sting?
    Where, grave, your victory?
  I triumph still if you abide with me.

5 Hold now your cross before my closing eyes;
  shine through the gloom
    and point me to the skies!
  Heaven's morning breaks
    and earth's vain shadows flee:
  in life, in death, O Lord, abide with me!

4

Charles Wesley
© in this version Jubilate Hymns

1 All creation join to say:
  Christ the Lord is risen today!
  raise your joys and triumphs high;
  sing, you heavens, and earth reply:
    Alleluia!

2 Love's redeeming work is done;
  fought the fight, the battle won:
  see, our Sun's eclipse has passed;
  see, the dawn has come at last!
    Alleluia!

3 Vain the stone, the watch, the seal:
  Christ has burst the gates of hell;
  death in vain forbids his rise –
  Christ has opened paradise:
    Alleluia!

4 Now he lives, our glorious king;
  now, O death, where is your sting?
  Once he died, our souls to save –
  where's your victory, boasting grave?
    Alleluia!

5 So we rise where Christ has led,
  following our exalted head;
  made like him, like him we rise –
  ours the cross, the grave, the skies:
    Alleluia!

6 Hail the Lord of earth and heaven!
  praise to you by both be given;
  every knee to you shall bow,
  risen Christ, triumphant now:
    Alleluia!

5 After Francis of Assisi
William Draper
© in this version Jubilate Hymns

1 All creatures of our God and King,
  lift up your voice and with us sing:
    Alleluia, alleluia!
  Bright burning sun with golden beam,
  soft shining moon with silver gleam,
    O praise him, O praise him,
    Alleluia, alleluia, alleluia!

2 Swift rushing wind so wild and strong,
  white clouds that sail in heaven along,
    O praise him, alleluia!
  New rising dawn in praise rejoice,
  you lights of evening find a voice;
    O praise him . . .

3 Cool flowing water, pure and clear,
  make music for your Lord to hear:
    Alleluia, alleluia!
  Fierce fire so masterful and bright
  giving to us both warmth and light,
    O praise him . . .

4 Earth ever fertile, day by day
  bring forth your blessings on our way,
    O praise him, alleluia!
  All fruit and crops that richly grow,
  all trees and flowers God's glory show;
    O praise him . . .

5 People and nations, take your part,
  love and forgive with all your heart.
    Alleluia, alleluia!
  All who long pain and sorrow bear,
  trust God and cast on him your care;
    O praise him . . .

6 Death, once the ancient enemy,
  hear now our Easter melody,
    O praise him, alleluia!
  You are the pathway home to God,
  our door to life through Christ our Lord:
    O praise him . . .

7 Let all things their Creator bless
  and worship him in lowliness:
    Alleluia, alleluia!
  Praise, praise the Father, praise the Son,
  and praise the Spirit, Three-in-One,
    O praise him . . .

6 After Theodulph, John Neale
© in this version Jubilate Hymns

  All glory, praise and honour,
  to you, redeemer, king,
  to whom the lips of children
  made sweet hosannas ring.

1 You are the king of Israel,
  great David's greater son;
  you ride in lowly triumph,
  the Lord's anointed one!
    All glory, praise . . .

2 The company of angels
  are praising you on high,
  and we with all creation
  together make reply:
    All glory, praise . . .

3 The people of the Hebrews
  with palms before you went;
  our praise and prayer and anthems
  before you we present.
    All glory, praise . . .

4 To you before your passion
  they sang their hymns of praise;
  to you, now high exalted,
  our melody we raise:
    All glory, praise . . .

5 As you received their praises,
  accept the prayers we bring:
  for you delight in goodness,
  O good and gracious king!
    All glory, praise . . .

Verses 2 and 4 may be omitted

7 After Edward Perronet and John Rippon
© in this version Jubilate Hymns

1 All hail the power of Jesus' name!
  Let kings before him fall,
  his might and majesty proclaim
  and crown him Lord of all.

2 Come, crown him, moon and stars of night:
  he made you, great and small.
  Bright sun, praise him who gave you light,
  and crown him Lord of all.

3 Crown him, you martyrs spurning pain,
  who witnessed to his call;
  now sing your victory-song again
  and crown him Lord of all.

4 Let all who trust in Christ exclaim
  in wonder, to recall
  the one who bore our sin and shame,
  and crown him Lord of all.

5 Then in that final judgement hour
  when all rebellions fall,
  we'll rise in his triumphant power
  and crown him Lord of all.

8 After Paul Gerhardt, Catherine Winkworth
© in this version Word & Music / Jubilate Hymns

1 All my heart this night rejoices,
    as I hear,
    far and near,
  sweetest angel voices.
  'Christ is born!' their choirs are singing,
    till the air
    everywhere
  now with joy is ringing.

2 Listen! from a humble manger
    comes the call,
    'One and all,
  run from sin and danger!
  Christians come, let nothing grieve you:
    you are freed!
    All you need
  I will surely give you.'

3 Gather, then, from every nation;
    hére let all,
    great and small,
  kneel in adoration;
  love him who with love is yearning;
    hail the star
    that from far
  bright with hope is burning!

4 You, my Lord, with love I'll cherish,
    live to you,
    and with you
  dying, shall not perish,
  but shall dwell with you for ever:
    joy divine
    shall be mine
  that can alter never.

9 From Psalm 100, William Kethe
© in this version Jubilate Hymns

1 All people that on earth do dwell,
  sing to the Lord with cheerful voice;
  serve him with joy, his praises tell,
  come now before him and rejoice!

2 Know that the Lord is God indeed,
  he formed us all without our aid;
  we are the flock he loves to feed,
  the sheep who by his hand are made.

3 O enter then his gates with praise,
  and in his courts his love proclaim;
  give thanks and bless him all your days:
  let every tongue confess his name.

4 For God our mighty Lord is good,
  his mercy is for ever sure;
  his truth at all times firmly stood,
  and shall from age to age endure.

5 Praise God the Father, God the Son,
  and God the Spirit evermore;
  all praise to God the Three-in-One –
  let heaven rejoice and earth adore!

Verse 5 is omitted when using the second tune

10 © Timothy Dudley-Smith

1 All shall be well!
  for on our Easter skies
  see Christ the Sun of Righteousness arise.

2 All shall be well!
  the sacrifice is made;
  the sinner freed, the price of pardon paid.

3 All shall be well!
  the cross and passion past;
  dark night is done,
    bright morning come at last.

4 All shall be well!
  Lift every voice on high,
  'Death has no more dominion, but shall die.'

5 Jesus alive!
  rejoice and sing again,
  'All shall be well for evermore, Amen!
  All shall be well for evermore, Amen!'

11 Cecil Alexander

  All things bright and beautiful,
  all creatures great and small;
  all things wise and wonderful –
  the Lord God made them all.

1 Each little flower that opens,
  each little bird that sings –
  he made their glowing colours,
  he made their tiny wings.
    All things bright . . .

2 The purple-headed mountain,
  the river running by,
  the sunset, and the morning
  that brightens up the sky:
    All things bright . . .

3 The cold wind in the winter,
the pleasant summer sun,
the ripe fruits in the garden –
he made them every one.
    All things bright and beautiful,
    all creatures great and small;
    all things wise and wonderful –
    the Lord God made them all.

4 He gave us eyes to see them,
and lips that we might tell
how great is God almighty,
who has made all things well!
    All things bright . . .

12 Job Hupton and John Neale
© in this version Jubilate Hymns

1 Alleluia! Raise the anthem,
let the skies resound with praise;
sing to Christ who brought salvation:
wonderful his works and ways –
God eternal, Word incarnate,
whom the heaven of heavens obeys.

2 Long before he formed the mountains,
spread the seas or made the sky,
love eternal, free and boundless,
moved the Lord of life to die;
fore-ordained the Prince of princes
for the throne of Calvary.

3 There for us and our redemption
see him all his life-blood pour:
there he wins our full salvation,
dies that we may die no more –
then arising lives for ever,
King of kings, whom we adore.

4 Praise and honour to the Father,
praise and honour to the Son,
praise and honour to the Spirit,
ever Three and ever One:
one in grace and one in glory
while eternal ages run!

13 William Dix

1 Alleluia, sing to Jesus!
his the sceptre, his the throne:
Alleluia! – his the triumph,
his the victory alone.
Hear the songs of holy Zion
thunder like a mighty flood:
'Jesus out of every nation
has redeemed us by his blood!'

2 Alleluia! – not as orphans
are we left in sorrow now:
Alleluia! – he is near us;
faith believes, nor questions how.
Though the cloud from sight received him
whom the angels now adore,
shall our hearts forget his promise,
'I am with you evermore'?

3 Alleluia! – bread of heaven,
here on earth our food, our stay:
Alleluia! – here the sinful
come to you from day to day.
Intercessor, friend of sinners,
earth's redeemer, plead for me,
where the songs of all the sinless
sweep across the crystal sea.

4 Alleluia, sing to Jesus!
his the sceptre, his the throne:
Alleluia! – his the triumph,
his the victory alone.
Hear the songs of holy Zion
thunder like a mighty flood:
'Jesus out of every nation
has redeemed us by his blood!'

14 From *The Alternative Service Book 1980*
adapted Christopher Rolinson
© 1980 Central Board of Finance of the Church of England

Almighty God, our heavenly Father,
we have sinned against you,
in thought and word and deed,
in thought and word and deed,
through negligence, through weakness,
through our own deliberate fault.

We are truly sorry
and repent of all our sins.
For the sake of your Son, Jesus Christ,
    who died for us,
    who died for us,
    who died for us,
forgive us all that is past;
and grant that we may serve you
in newness of life
A   to the glory of your name,
B   to the glory of your name,
A   to the glory of your name,
B   to the glory of your name,
ALL   to the glory of your name.

Amen, amen.

The congregation may divide at A and B

15 From *The Alternative Service Book 1980*
© 1980 Central Board of Finance of the Church of England

Almighty God, we thank you for feeding us
with the body and blood of your Son,
    Jesus Christ.
Through him we offer you
    our souls and bodies
to be a living sacrifice.
Send us out in the power of your Spirit
to live and work to your praise and glory.

Almighty God . . . Amen, amen, amen.

16 John Newton
© in this version Jubilate Hymns

1 Amazing grace – how sweet the sound –
    that saved a wretch like me!
    I once was lost, but now am found;
    was blind, but now I see.

2 God's grace first taught my heart to fear,
    his grace my fears relieved:
    how precious did that grace appear
    the hour I first believed!

3 Through every danger, trial and snare
    I have already come;
    for grace has brought me safe thus far,
    and grace will lead me home.

4 The Lord has promised good to me,
    his word my hope secures;
    my shield and stronghold he shall be
    as long as life endures.

5 And when this earthly life is past,
    and mortal cares shall cease,
    I shall possess with Christ at last
    eternal joy and peace.

17 Charles Wesley
© in this version Jubilate Hymns

1 And can it be that I should gain
    an interest in the Saviour's blood?
    Died he for me, who caused his pain;
    for me, who him to death pursued?
    Amazing love! – how can it be
    that you, my God, should die for me?

2 What mystery here! – the Immortal dies;
    who can explore his strange design?
    In vain the first-born seraph tries
    to sound the depths of love divine.
    Such mercy this! – let earth adore;
    let angel minds inquire no more.

3 He left his Father's throne above –
    so free, so infinite his grace –
    emptied himself of all but love,
    and bled for Adam's helpless race.
    What mercy this, immense and free,
    for, O my God, it found out me!

4 Long my imprisoned spirit lay,
    fast bound in sin and nature's night:
    your sunrise turned that night to day;
    I woke – the dungeon flamed with light.
    My chains fell off, my heart was free;
    I rose, went out to liberty!

5 No condemnation now I dread;
    Jesus, and all in him, is mine!
    Alive in him, my living head,
    and clothed in righteousness divine,
    bold I approach the eternal throne
    and claim the crown through Christ my own.

Traditional Version

1 And can it be that I should gain
    an interest in the Saviour's blood?
    Died he for me, who caused his pain;
    for me, who him to death pursued?
    Amazing love! – how can it be
    that thou, my God, shouldst die for me?

2 'Tis mystery all! – the Immortal dies, –
    who can explore his strange design?
    In vain the first-born seraph tries
    to sound the depths of love divine!
    'Tis mercy all! – Let earth adore;
    let angel minds inquire no more.

3 He left his Father's throne above –
    so free, so infinite his grace –
    emptied himself of all but love,
    and bled for Adam's helpless race.
    'Tis mercy all, immense and free;
    for, O my God, it found out me.

4 Long my imprisoned spirit lay
    fast bound in sin and nature's night:
    thine eye diffused a quickening ray;
    I woke – the dungeon flamed with light.
    My chains fell off, my heart was free;
    I rose, went forth, and followed thee.

5 No condemnation now I dread;
    Jesus, and all in him, is mine!
    Alive in him, my living head,
    and clothed in righteousness divine,
    bold I approach the eternal throne
    and claim the crown through Christ my own.

18
Francis Pott
© in this version Jubilate Hymns

1 Angel voices ever singing
   round your throne of light,
angels' music ever ringing
   rests not day or night:
thousands only live to bless you
   and confess you Lord of might.

2 Lord beyond our mortal sight,
   in glory far away,
can it be that you delight
   in sinners' songs today;
may we know that you are near us
   and will hear us? Yes, we may!

3 Yes, we know your heart rejoices
   in each work divine,
using minds and hands and voices
   in your great design;
craftsman's art and music's measure
   for your pleasure all combine.

4 Here to you, great God, we offer
   praise in harmony,
and for your acceptance proffer
   all unworthily
hearts and minds and hands and voices
   in our choicest psalmody.

5 Honour, glory, might and merit
   for your works and ways,
Father, Son and Holy Spirit,
   God through endless days;
with the best that you have given
   earth and heaven render praise.

19
James Montgomery
© in this version Jubilate Hymns

1 Angels from the realms of glory,
wing your flight through all the earth;
heralds of creation's story,
now proclaim Messiah's birth!
   Come and worship
   Christ, the new-born king;
   come and worship,
   worship Christ
   the new-born king.

2 Shepherds in the fields abiding,
watching by your flocks at night:
God with us is now residing –
see, there shines the infant light!
   Come and worship . . .

3 Wise men, leave your contemplations!
Brighter visions shine afar:
seek in him the hope of nations,
you have seen his rising star:
   Come and worship . . .

4 Though an infant now we view him,
he will share his Father's throne,
gather all the nations to him;
every knee shall then bow down:
   Come and worship . . .

20
© Timothy Dudley-Smith

1 As water to the thirsty,
as beauty to the eyes,
as strength that follows weakness,
as truth instead of lies,
as songtime and springtime
and summertime to be,
   so is my Lord,
   my living Lord,
so is my Lord to me.

2 Like calm in place of clamour,
like peace that follows pain,
like meeting after parting,
like sunshine after rain,
like moonlight and starlight
and sunlight on the sea,
   so is my Lord,
   my living Lord,
so is my Lord to me.

3 As sleep that follows fever,
as gold instead of grey,
as freedom after bondage,
as sunrise to the day;
as home to the traveller
and all we long to see,
   so is my Lord,
   my living Lord,
so is my Lord to me.

21
William Dix
© in this version Jubilate Hymns

1 As with gladness men of old
did the guiding star behold,
as with joy they hailed its light,
leading onward, beaming bright:
so, most gracious Lord, may we
evermore your splendour see.

2 As with joyful steps they sped
    to that lowly manger bed,
    there to bend the knee before
    Christ whom heaven and earth adore:
    so with ever-quickening pace
    may we seek your throne of grace.

3 As they offered gifts most rare
    at your cradle plain and bare,
    so may we with holy joy
    pure and free from sin's alloy,
    all our costliest treasures bring,
    Christ, to you, our heavenly king.

4 Holy Jesus, every day
    keep us in the narrow way,
    and when earthly things are past,
    bring our ransomed souls at last:
    where they need no star to guide,
    where no clouds your glory hide.

5 In the heavenly country bright
    none shall need created light –
    you, its light, its joy, its crown,
    you its sun which goes not down;
    there for ever shall we sing
    alleluias to our king.

22

Caroline Noel
© in this version Jubilate Hymns

1 At the name of Jesus
    every knee shall bow,
  every tongue confess him
    king of glory now;
  this the Father's pleasure,
    that we call him Lord,
  who from the beginning
    was the mighty Word.

2 At his voice creation
    sprang at once to sight,
  all the angel faces,
    all the hosts of light;
  thrones and dominations,
    stars upon their way,
  all the heavenly orders,
    in the great array.

3 Humbled for a season,
    to receive a name
  from the lips of sinners
    unto whom he came;
  faithfully he bore it
    spotless to the last,
  brought it back victorious
    when from death he passed:

4 Bore it up triumphant
    with its human light,
  through all ranks of creatures
    to the central height;
  to the eternal Godhead,
    to the Father's throne,
  filled it with the glory
    of his triumph won.

5 Name him, Christians, name him,
    with love strong as death,
  but with awe and wonder,
    and with bated breath;
  he is God the saviour,
    he is Christ the Lord,
  ever to be worshipped,
    trusted and adored.

6 In your hearts enthrone him;
    there let him subdue
  all that is not holy,
    all that is not true;
  crown him as your captain
    in temptation's hour,
  let his will enfold you
    in its light and power.

7 With his Father's glory
    Jesus comes again,
  angel hosts attend him
    and announce his reign;
  for all wreaths of empire
    meet upon his brow,
  and our hearts confess him
    king of glory now.

Verses 2 and 6 may be omitted

23

From Revelation 1, Dave Fellingham
© 1982 Thankyou Music

1 At your feet we fall, mighty risen Lord,
  as we come before your throne
    to worship you!
  By your Spirit's power
    you now draw our hearts,
  and we hear your voice
    in triumph ringing clear:
  'I am he who lives,
  who lives and was dead:
  behold I am alive –
  for evermore!'

2 There we see you stand, mighty risen Lord,
  clothed in garments pure and holy,
        shining bright;
  eyes of flashing fire,
        feet like burnished bronze,
  and the sound of many waters is your voice.
      'I am he who lives,
      who lives and was dead:
      behold I am alive –
      for evermore!'

3 Like the shining sun in its noon-day strength,
  we now see the glory of your wondrous face:
  once that face was marred,
        but now you're glorified;
  and your words, like a two-edged sword,
        have mighty power.
      'I am he that lives . . .

24 Verses 1, 2 unknown
      verse 3 John MacFarland

1 Away in a manger, no crib for a bed,
  the little Lord Jesus laid down his sweet head;
  the stars in the bright sky
        looked down where he lay;
  the little Lord Jesus asleep on the hay.

2 The cattle are lowing, the baby awakes,
  but little Lord Jesus no crying he makes:
  I love you, Lord Jesus –
        look down from on high
  and stay by my side until morning is nigh.

3 Be near me, Lord Jesus; I ask you to stay
  close by me for ever and love me, I pray;
  bless all the dear children in your tender care,
  and fit us for heaven to live with you there.

25 © Michael Saward / Jubilate Hymns

1 Baptised in water,
  sealed by the Spirit,
  cleansed by the blood of Christ our king;
  heirs of salvation,
  trusting his promise –
  faithfully now God's praise we sing.

2 Baptised in water,
  sealed by the Spirit,
  dead in the tomb with Christ our king;
  one with his rising,
  freed and forgiven
  thankfully now God's praise we sing.

3 Baptised in water,
  sealed by the Spirit,
  marked with the sign of Christ our king;
  born of one Father,
  we are his children –
  joyfully now God's praise we sing.

26 David Evans
      © 1986 Thankyou Music

1 Be still,
  for the presence of the Lord,
      the holy One, is here;
  come bow before him now
  with reverence and fear:
  in him no sin is found –
  we stand on holy ground.
  Be still,
  for the presence of the Lord,
      the holy One, is here.

2 Be still,
  for the glory of the Lord
      is shining all around;
  he burns with holy fire,
  with splendour he is crowned:
  how awesome is the sight –
  our radiant king of light!
  Be still,
  for the glory of the Lord
      is shining all around.

3 Be still,
  for the power of the Lord
      is moving in this place:
  he comes to cleanse and heal,
  to minister his grace –
  no work too hard for him.
  In faith receive from him.
  Be still,
  for the power of the Lord
      is moving in this place.

27 From Psalm 23
      © 1985 Christopher Walker
      published by Oregon Catholic Press

1 Because the Lord is my shepherd
  I have everything I need;
  he lets me rest in the meadow
  and leads me to the quiet streams;
  he restores my soul
  and he leads me in the paths that are right.
      Lord, you are my shepherd,
      you are my friend:
      I want to follow you always –
      just to follow my friend.

2 And when the road leads to darkness,
   I shall walk there unafraid;
   even when death is close
   I have courage, for your help is there;
   you are close beside me with comfort,
   you are guiding my way.
       Lord, you are my shepherd . . .

3 In love you make me a banquet
   for my enemies to see;
   you make me welcome,
   pouring down honour
       from your mighty hand;
   and this joy fills me with gladness –
   it is too much to bear.
       Lord, you are my shepherd . . .

4 Your goodness always is with me,
   and your mercy I know;
   your loving-kindness strengthens me always
   as I go through life;
   I shall dwell in your presence for ever,
   giving praise to your name.
       Lord, you are my shepherd . . .

28 © Judy Davies / Jubilate Hymns

1 Bless the Lord, created things,
   highest heavens, angel host;
   bless the Father, Spirit, Son:
       worship, all creation.

2 Sun and moon and stars of heaven,
   showery waters, rain and dew,
   stormy gale and fiery heat:
       worship, all creation.

3 Scorching wind and bitter cold,
   icy blizzard, morning mist,
   light and darkness, nights and days:
       worship, all creation.

4 Frosty air and falling snow,
   clouds and lightnings, dales and hills,
   all that grows upon the earth:
       worship, all creation.

5 Springs and rivers, ocean deeps,
   whales and fishes of the sea,
   prowling beasts and soaring birds:
       worship, all creation.

6 All on earth who serve our God,
   priestly people of the Lord,
   upright, holy, humble hearts:
       worship, all creation.

29 From Philippians 2 / © Brian Black and Word & Music / Jubilate Hymns

1 Before the heaven and earth
   were made by God's decree,
   the Son of God all-glorious dwelt
   in God's eternity.

2 Though in the form of God
   and rich beyond compare,
   he did not think to grasp his prize;
   nor did he linger there.

3 From heights of heaven he came
   to this world full of sin,
   to meet with hunger, hatred, hell –
   our life, our love to win.

4 The Son became true Man
   and took a servant's role;
   in lowliness and selfless love
   he came, to make us whole.

5 Obedient to his death –
   that death upon a cross,
   no son had ever shown such love,
   nor father known such loss.

6 To him enthroned on high,
   by angel hosts adored,
   all knees shall bow, and tongues confess
   that Jesus Christ is Lord.

30 John Keble and William Hall

1 Blessed are the pure in heart,
   for they shall see our God;
   the secret of the Lord is theirs,
   their soul is Christ's abode.

2 The Lord, who left the heavens
   our life and peace to bring;
   to dwell in lowliness with us,
   our pattern and our king:

3 Still to the lowly soul
   himself he will impart;
   and for his dwelling and his throne
   chooses the pure in heart.

4 Lord, we your presence seek:
   our inner life renew;
   give us a pure and lowly heart,
   a temple fit for you.

31 From Psalm 98, Joel 2 etc.
© Michael Perry / Jubilate Hymns

1 Blow upon the trumpet!
clap your hands together,
sound aloud the praises of the Lord
       your king.
He has kept his promise,
granting us salvation:
let his people jubilantly shout and sing!

2 Blow upon the trumpet!
let the nations tremble;
see his power obliterate the sun and moon.
This is God's own army
bringing all to judgement,
for the day of Jesus Christ is coming soon.

3 Blow upon the trumpet!
arrows in the lightning
fly the storm of battle where he marches on.
Glory to our shepherd
keeping us through danger,
setting us like jewels in his royal crown.

4 Blow upon the trumpet!
Christ is surely coming,
heaven's forces mobilizing at his word.
We shall rise to meet him:
death at last is conquered,
God gives us the victory
       through Christ our Lord!

The congregation repeats each line after the worship leader

32 © Brian Hoare / Jubilate Hymns

1 Born in song!
God's people have always been singing.
Born in song!
hearts and voices raised.
So today we worship together:
God alone is worthy to be praised.

2 Christ is king!
he left the glory of heaven.
Christ is king!
born to share in our pain;
crucified, for sinners atoning;
risen, exalted, soon to come again.

3 Sing the song!
God's Spirit is poured out among us.
Sing the song!
God has made us anew;
every member part of the Body,
given his power, his will to seek and do.

4 Tell the world!
all power to Jesus is given.
Tell the world!
he is with us always.
Spread the word, that all may receive him;
every tongue confess and sing his praise.

5 Then the end!
Christ Jesus shall reign in his glory.
Then the end
of all earthly days.
Yet above, the song will continue;
all his people still shall sing his praise!

33 © Michael Perry / Jubilate Hymns

1 Born of the water,
born of the Spirit –
    called by the wind and the fire;
sealed with his promise,
we shall inherit
    more than the most we desire.

2 One through redemption,
one with the Father –
    children of grace and of heaven;
joyfully sharing
faith with each other,
    sinners whose sins are forgiven.

3 Glory, all glory,
glory to Jesus –
    die we in him and we live!
friends for his service,
heirs to the treasures
    God, and God only, can give.

34 Reginald Heber

1 Bread of the world in mercy broken,
wine of the soul in mercy shed;
by whom the words of life were spoken
and in whose death our sins are dead:

2 Look on the heart by sorrow broken,
look on the tears by sinners shed,
and make your feast to us the token
that by your grace our souls are fed.

35
Mary Lathbury and Alexander Groves
© in this version Word and Music / Jubilate Hymns

1 Break now the bread of life,
    dear Lord, to me
as you once broke the bread
    beside the sea:
beyond the sacred page
    I seek you, Lord;
my spirit longs for you,
    the living Word.

2 You are the bread of life,
    O Lord, to me;
your holy word, your truth,
    is food for me:
grant I may eat and live
    with you above;
teach me to love your truth,
    for you are love.

3 Now send your Spirit, Lord,
    to strengthen me,
so let him touch my eyes
    that I may see:
show me the truth concealed
    within your word;
so in your love revealed
    I'll see you, Lord.

4 Bless now the bread of life
    to me, to me,
as you once blessed the loaves
    by Galilee:
then shall all bondage cease,
    all fetters fall,
and I shall find my peace,
    my all in all.

36
Edwin Hatch
© in this version Jubilate Hymns

1 Breathe on me, breath of God;
fill me with life anew,
your love be mine in all I love,
your power in all I do.

2 Breathe on me, breath of God,
until my heart is pure,
until my will is one with yours
to do and to endure.

3 Breathe on me, breath of God;
fulfil my heart's desire,
until this earthly part of me
glows with your heavenly fire.

4 Breathe on me, breath of God:
so shall I never die,
but live with you the perfect life
of your eternity.

37
From Psalms 149 and 150
© Michael Perry / Jubilate Hymns

1 Bring to the Lord a glad new song,
children of grace extol your king:
your love and praise to God belong –
to instruments of music, sing!
Let those be warned who spurn God's name,
let rulers all obey his word:
God's justice shall bring tyrants shame –
let every creature praise the Lord!

2 Sing praise within these hallowed walls,
worship beneath the dome of heaven;
by cymbals' sounds and trumpets' calls
let praises fit for God be given:
with strings and brass and wind rejoice –
then, join our song in full accord
all living things with breath and voice;
let every creature praise the Lord!

38
Janet Lunt
© 1978 Sovereign Lifestyle Music UK

    Broken for me, broken for you,
    the body of Jesus broken for you.

1 He offered his body, he poured out his soul,
Jesus was broken that we might be whole:
    Broken for me . . .

2 Come to my table and with me dine,
eat of my bread and drink of my wine:
    Broken for me . . .

3 This is my body given for you,
eat it remembering I died for you:
    Broken for me . . .

4 This is my blood I shed for you,
for your forgiveness, making you new:
    Broken for me . . .

39
After Mary MacDonald
Lachlan Macbean

1 Child in the manger, infant of Mary,
outcast and stranger, Lord of all!
child who inherits all our transgressions,
all our demerits on him fall.

2 Once the most holy child of salvation
gentle and lowly lived below:
now as our glorious mighty redeemer,
see him victorious over each foe.

3 Prophets foretold him, infant of wonder;
angels behold him on his throne:
worthy our saviour of all their praises;
happy for ever are his own.

40

1 Christ in majesty ascending!
Christ in splendour reigns on high;
at God's throne, in praise unending,
heaven's hosts 'hosanna' cry.
With that song our voices blending
Christ our king we glorify.

2 Christ triumphant there is seated
and the race of faith is run;
now redemption is completed,
love's great victory is won.
Shall not now the world be greeted
with the gospel of God's Son?

3 Christ his promise swift fulfilling
sends his Spirit for the task;
wisdom, patience, grace instilling –
gifts we scarcely dare to ask.
So shall Christian lives, God willing,
faith awaken, sin unmask.

4 Christ ascending! Christ preparing
an eternal dwelling-place;
there our human nature wearing,
representing every race.
At the last, Christ's splendour sharing,
we shall see the Father's face.

41

1 Christ is alive! let Christians sing:
the cross stands empty to the sky.
Let streets and homes with praises ring:
Love, drowned in death, shall never die.

2 Christ is alive! no longer bound
to distant years in Palestine,
but saving, healing here and now,
and touching every place and time.

3 Not throned afar, remotely high,
untouched, unmoved by human pains,
but daily, in the midst of life,
our Saviour in the God-head reigns.

4 In every insult, rift and war,
where colour, scorn or wealth divide,
Christ suffers still, yet loves the more,
and lives where even hope has died.

5 Christ is alive, and comes to bring
good news to this and every age,
till earth and sky and ocean ring
with joy, with justice, love, and praise.

42

1 Christ is ascending! let creation sing:
suffering is ending, now Christ rules as king.
Friends who stand disheartened
    soon are helped to know
Christ shall come in glory, as they see him go.
    Christ is ascending, let creation sing:
    suffering is ending,
    now Christ rules as king.

2 Watch the outpouring from our Lord above,
Pentecost restoring faith and hope and love;
brothers shall see visions, sisters prophesy,
sun and stars be darkened,
    wonders fill the sky!
    Christ is ascending . . .

3 Come, Holy Spirit, strengthen us today:
let us each inherit gifts from Christ, we pray;
not for praise by others,
    but that they may give
glory to the Father by whose power we live!
    Christ is ascending . . .

43

1 Christ is going to the Father:
heaven and hell and earth, attend!
Marked by blood, in death made perfect,
see the Man to God ascend.
Love was captured, cursed and murdered:
in the losing, love has won;
in the dying, love has risen,
by its ruin, gained a throne.

2 Christ is going to the Father
from the world he came to save,
bringing life to those who listen,
raised in wonder from their grave.
Eldest of a new creation,
Head of all, he leads the way,
calling, drawing us to follow,
sharing his ascension day.

3 Christ is going to the Father:
hear a newborn nation cry –
earth renewed by heaven's music,
Glory be to God on high!
Sing Hosanna, all believers;
Hallelujah, shout his name:
Jesus, universal Saviour,
all the universe proclaim.

44 John Neale
© in this version Jubilate Hymns

1 Christ is made the sure foundation,
  Christ the head and corner-stone
  chosen of the Lord and precious,
  binding all the Church in one;
  holy Zion's help for ever,
  and her confidence alone.

2 All within that holy city
  dearly loved of God on high,
  in exultant jubilation
  sing, in perfect harmony;
  God the One-in-Three adoring
  in glad hymns eternally.

3 We as living stones implore you:
  Come among us, Lord, today!
  with your gracious loving-kindness
  hear your children as we pray;
  and the fulness of your blessing
  in our fellowship display.

4 Here entrust to all your servants
  what we long from you to gain –
  that on earth and in the heavens
  we one people shall remain,
  till united in your glory
  evermore with you we reign.

5 Praise and honour to the Father,
  praise and honour to the Son,
  praise and honour to the Spirit,
  ever Three and ever One:
  one in power and one in glory
  while eternal ages run.

45 Christopher Rolinson
© 1989 Thankyou Music

  Christ is risen!
  Alleluia, alleluia!
  Christ is risen!
  Risen indeed, alleluia!

1 Love's work is done,
  the battle is won.
  Where now, O death, is your sting?
  He rose again
  to rule and to reign,
  Jesus our conquering king.
    Christ is risen . . .

2 Lord over sin,
  Lord over death,
  at his feet Satan must fall!
  Every knee, bow!
  All will confess
  Jesus is Lord over all!
    Christ is risen . . .

3 Tell it abroad,
  'Jesus is Lord!'
  Shout it and let your praise ring!
  Gladly we raise
  our songs of praise –
  worship is our offering.
    Christ is risen . . .

46 From Revelation 22
© Christopher Idle / Jubilate Hymns

1 Christ is surely coming
    bringing his reward,
  omega and alpha,
    first and last and Lord;
  root and stem of David,
    brilliant morning star –
  Meet your judge and saviour,
    nations near and far;
  meet your judge and saviour,
    nations near and far!

2 See the holy city!
    There they enter in,
  all by Christ made holy,
    washed from every sin;
  thirsty ones, desiring
    all he loves to give:
  Come for living water,
    freely drink, and live;
  come for living water,
    freely drink, and live!

3 Grace be with God's people!
    Praise his holy name –
  Father, Son, and Spirit,
    evermore the same!
  Hear the certain promise
    from the eternal home:
  'Surely I come quickly!' –
    Come, Lord Jesus, come;
  'Surely I come quickly!' –
    Come, Lord Jesus, come!

47 George Bell
© Oxford University Press

1 Christ is the king! O friends rejoice;
  brothers and sisters, with one voice
  let the world know he is your choice.
    Alleluia, alleluia, alleluia!

2 O magnify the Lord, and raise
  anthems of joy and holy praise
  for Christ's brave saints of ancient days.
    Alleluia . . .

3 They with a faith for ever new
   followed the king, and round him drew
   thousands of faithful friends and true.
      Alleluia, alleluia, alleluia!

4 O Christian women, Christian men,
   all the world over, seek again
   the way disciples followed then.
      Alleluia . . .

5 Christ through all ages is the same:
   place the same hope in his great name;
   with the same faith his word proclaim.
      Alleluia . . .

6 Let Love's unconquerable might
   your scattered companies unite
   in service to the Lord of light.
      Alleluia . . .

7 So shall God's will on earth be done,
   new lamps be lit, new tasks begun,
   and the whole church at last be one.
      Alleluia . . .

48 Frederick Pratt Green
© Stainer & Bell Ltd

1 Christ is the world's Light,
      he and none other;
   born in our darkness,
      he became our Brother –
   if we have seen him, we have seen the Father:
      Glory to God on high!

2 Christ is the world's Peace,
      he and none other;
   no one can serve him;
      and despise another –
   who else unites us, one in God the Father?
      Glory to God on high!

3 Christ is the world's Life, he and none other;
   sold once for silver, murdered here,
      our Brother –
   he, who redeems us, reigns with the Father:
      Glory to God on high!

4 Give God the glory, God and none other;
   give God the glory, Spirit, Son and Father;
   give God the glory, God in Man my brother:
      Glory to God on high!

49 After Michael Weisse
Catherine Winkworth

1 Christ the Lord is risen again,
   Christ has broken every chain;
   hear the angel voices cry,
   singing evermore on high:
      Alleluia!

2 He who gave for us his life,
   who for us endured the strife,
   is our paschal lamb today;
   we too sing for joy and say:
      Alleluia!

3 He who bore all pain and loss
   comfortless upon the cross
   lives in glory now on high,
   pleads for us and hears our cry:
      Alleluia!

4 He who slumbered in the grave
   is exalted now to save;
   through the universe it rings
   that the lamb is King of kings:
      Alleluia!

5 Now he bids us tell abroad
   how the lost may be restored,
   how the penitent forgiven,
   how we too may enter heaven:
      Alleluia!

6 Christ, our paschal lamb indeed,
   all your ransomed people feed!
   Take our sins and guilt away;
   let us sing by night and day:
      Alleluia!

50 © Michael Saward / Jubilate Hymns

1 Christ triumphant, ever reigning,
   Saviour, Master, King!
   Lord of heaven, our lives sustaining,
   hear us as we sing:
      Yours the glory and the crown,
      the high renown,
      the eternal name.

2 Word incarnate, truth revealing,
   Son of Man on earth!
   power and majesty concealing
   by your humble birth:
      Yours the glory . . .

3 Suffering servant, scorned, ill-treated,
   victim crucified!
   death is through the cross defeated,
   sinners justified:
      Yours the glory . . .

4 Priestly king, enthroned for ever
   high in heaven above!
   sin and death and hell shall never
   stifle hymns of love:
      Yours the glory . . .

5 So, our hearts and voices raising
   through the ages long,
   ceaselessly upon you gazing,
   this shall be our song:
       Yours the glory . . .

51 Charles Wesley

1 Christ whose glory fills the skies,
   Christ the true, the only light;
   Sun of righteousness, arise,
   triumph over shades of night:
       Dayspring from on high, be near;
       Daystar, in my heart appear!

2 Dark and cheerless is the dawn
   till your mercy's beams I see;
   joyless is the day's return
   till your glories shine on me:
       as they inward light impart,
       cheer my eyes and warm my heart.

3 Visit then this soul of mine,
   pierce the gloom of sin and grief;
   fill me, radiancy divine,
   scatter all my unbelief:
       more and more yourself display,
       shining to the perfect day!

52 Brian Wren

1 Christ upon the mountain peak
   stands alone in glory blazing;
   let us, if we dare to speak,
   with the saints and angels praise him –
       Alleluia! Alleluia!

2 Trembling at his feet we saw
   Moses and Elijah speaking:
   all the prophets and the law
   shout through them their joyful greeting –
       Alleluia! Alleluia!

3 Swift the cloud of glory came,
   God proclaiming in its thunder
   Jesus as his Son by name!
   nations, cry aloud in wonder –
       Alleluia! Alleluia!

4 This is God's belovèd Son!
   law and prophets fade before him,
   First and Last, and only One:
   let creation now adore him –
       Alleluia! Alleluia!

53 John Byrom

1 Christians, awake, salute the happy morn
   on which the saviour of the world was born;
   rise to adore the mystery of love
   which hosts of angels chanted from above!
   With them the joyful tidings first begun
   of God incarnate and the virgin's Son.

2 First, to the watchful shepherds it was told,
   who heard the herald angel's voice: 'Behold,
   I bring good news of your Messiah's birth
   to you and all the nations here on earth!
   This day has God fulfilled his promised word;
   this day is born a saviour, Christ the Lord!'

3 To Bethlehem these eager shepherds ran
   to see the wonder of our God made man;
   they found, with Joseph and the holy maid,
   her son, the saviour, in a manger laid.
   Amazed, with joy this story they proclaim,
   the first apostles of his infant fame.

4 Let us, like those good shepherds,
           now employ
   our grateful voices to declare the joy:
   Christ, who was born on this most happy day,
   round all the earth his glory shall display.
   Saved by his love, unceasing we shall sing
   eternal praise to heaven's almighty king.

54 From 1 Peter 2, James Seddon

1 Church of God, elect and glorious,
   holy nation, chosen race;
   called as God's own special people,
   royal priests and heirs of grace:
   know the purpose of your calling,
   show to all his mighty deeds;
   tell of love which knows no limits,
   grace which meets all human needs.

2 God has called you out of darkness
   into his most marvellous light;
   brought his truth to life within you,
   turned your blindness into sight.
   Let your light so shine around you
   that God's name is glorified;
   and all find fresh hope and purpose
   in Christ Jesus crucified.

3 Once you were an alien people,
   strangers to God's heart of love;
   but he brought you home in mercy,
   citizens of heaven above.
   Let his love flow out to others,
   let them feel a Father's care;
   that they too may know his welcome
   and his countless blessings share.

4 Church of God, elect and holy,
  be the people he intends;
  strong in faith and swift to answer
  each command your master sends:
  royal priests, fulfil your calling
  through your sacrifice and prayer;
  give your lives in joyful service –
  sing his praise, his love declare.

3 Choir and people, shout in wonder,
    Alleluia, gloria,
  let the merry organ thunder;
    alleluia, gloria,
  thank our God for love amazing,
    alleluia, gloria,
  Father, Son and Spirit praising.
    Alleluia, gloria!

55 From Psalm 93
© Michael Saward / Jubilate Hymns

1 Clothed in kingly majesty,
  robed in regal power,
    God is over all,
    God is over all.

2 Lord of all, secure and strong
  throned beyond all time,
    God is over all,
    God is over all.

3 Greater than the river's roar
  and the surging sea,
    God is over all,
    God is over all.

4 Changeless as his law's decrees,
  crowned our holy king,
    God is over all,
    God is over all.

57 Charles Wesley
© in this version Jubilate Hymns

1 Come, O long-expected Jesus,
  born to set your people free!
  From our fears and sins release us:
  Christ in whom our rest shall be.

2 Israel's strength and consolation,
  born salvation to impart;
  dear desire of every nation,
  joy of every longing heart:

3 Born your people to deliver,
  born a child and yet a king;
  born to reign in us for ever,
  now your gracious kingdom bring:

4 By your own eternal Spirit
  rule in all our hearts alone;
  by your all-sufficient merit
  raise us to your glorious throne!

56 © Michael Perry / Jubilate Hymns

1 Come and hear the joyful singing,
    Alleluia, gloria,
  set the bells of heaven ringing:
    alleluia, gloria,
  God the Lord has shown us favour –
    alleluia, gloria,
  Christ is born to be our saviour.
    Alleluia, gloria!

2 Angels of his birth are telling,
    Alleluia, gloria,
  prince of peace all powers excelling;
    alleluia, gloria,
  death and hell can not defeat him:
    alleluia, gloria,
  go to Bethlehem and greet him.
    Alleluia, gloria!

58 Graham Kendrick
© 1989 Make Way Music

1 Come and see, come and see,
  come and see the King of love;
  see the purple robe and crown of thorns
      he wears.
  Soldiers mock, rulers sneer,
  as he lifts the cruel cross;
  lone and friendless now
      he climbs towards the hill.
    We worship at your feet,
    where wrath and mercy meet,
    and a guilty world is washed
    by love's pure stream;
    for us he was made sin,
    O, help me take it in,
    deep wounds of love cry out
    'Father, forgive'.
    I worship, I worship,
    the Lamb who was slain.

2 Come and weep, come and mourn
for your sin that pierced him there;
so much deeper
than the wounds of thorn and nail.
All our pride, all our greed,
all our fallenness and shame;
and the Lord has laid the punishment on him.
We worship at your feet . . .

3 Man of heaven, born to earth
to restore us to your heaven,
here we bow in awe
beneath your searching eyes.
From your tears comes our joy,
from your death our life shall spring;
by your resurrection power we shall rise.
We worship at your feet . . .

59 From Revelation 4, 5
© Christopher Idle / Jubilate Hymns

1 Come and see the shining hope
that Christ's apostle saw;
on the earth, confusion,
but in heaven an open door,
where the living creatures
praise the Lamb for evermore:
Love has the victory for ever!
Amen, he comes! to bring his own reward!
Amen, praise God! for justice now restored;
kingdoms of the world become
the kingdoms of the Lord:
Love has the victory for ever!

2 All the gifts you send us, Lord,
are faithful, good and true;
holiness and righteousness
are shown in all you do:
who can see your greatest Gift
and fail to worship you?
Love has the victory for ever!
Amen, he comes . . .

3 Power and salvation
all belong to God on high!
So the mighty multitudes of heaven
make their cry,
singing Hallelujah where the echoes never die:
Love has the victory for ever!
Amen, he comes . . .

60 © Michael Perry / Jubilate Hymns

1 Come and sing the Christmas story
this holy night!
Christ is born: the hope of glory
dawns on our sight.
Alleluia! earth is ringing
with a thousand angels singing –
hear the message they are bringing
this holy night.

2 Jesus, Saviour, child of Mary this holy night,
in a world confused and weary
you are our light.
God is in a manger lying,
manhood taking, self denying,
life embracing, death defying this holy night.

3 Lord of all! Let us acclaim him
this holy night;
king of our salvation name him,
throned in the height.
Son of Man – let us adore him:
all the earth is waiting for him;
Son of God – we bow before him
this holy night.

61 After Bianco da Siena, Richard Littledale
© in this version Jubilate Hymns

1 Come down, O Love divine!
Seek out this soul of mine
and visit it with your own ardour glowing;
O Comforter, draw near,
within my heart appear,
and kindle it, your holy flame bestowing.

2 O let it freely burn
till earthly passions turn
to dust and ashes in its heat consuming;
and let your glorious light
shine ever on my sight,
and make my pathway clear, by your illuming.

3 Let holy charity
my outward vesture be,
and lowliness become my inner clothing;
true lowliness of heart
which takes the humbler part,
and for its own shortcomings
weeps with loathing.

4 And so the yearning strong
with which the soul will long
shall far surpass the power of human telling;
for none can guess its grace
till we become the place
in which the Holy Spirit makes his dwelling.

62 Isaac Watts

1 Come let us join our cheerful songs
with angels round the throne:
ten thousand thousand are their tongues,
but all their joys are one.

2 Worthy the Lamb who died, they cry,
to be exalted thus!
Worthy the Lamb, our lips reply,
for he was slain for us!

3 Jesus is worthy to receive
all praise and power divine;
and all the blessings we can give
with songs of heaven combine.

4 Let all who live beyond the sky,
the air and earth and seas
unite to lift his glory high
and sing his endless praise!

5 Let all creation join in one
to bless the sacred name
of him who reigns upon the throne,
and to adore the Lamb!

63 After Suzanne Toolan
Michael Baughen
© 1970, 1992 GIA Publications Inc.

1 Come, let us worship Christ
to the glory of God the Father,
for he is worthy of all our love;
he died and rose for us!
praise him as Lord and saviour.
    And when the trumpet shall sound
    and Jesus comes in great power,
    then he will raise us to be with him
    for evermore!

2 'I am the bread of life;
he who comes to me shall not hunger:
and all who trust in me shall not thirst' –
this is what Jesus said:
praise him as Lord and saviour.
    And when the trumpet . . .

3 'I am the door to life;
he who enters by me is saved,
abundant life he will then receive' –
this is what Jesus said:
praise him as Lord and saviour.
    And when the trumpet . . .

4 'I am the light of the world;
if you follow me, darkness ceases,
and in its place comes the light of life' –
this is what Jesus said:
praise him as Lord and saviour.
    And when the trumpet . . .

5 Lord, we are one with you;
we rejoice in your new creation:
our hearts are fired by your saving love –
take up our lives, O Lord,
and use us for your glory.
    And when the trumpet . . .

64 © 1990 Paul Inwood / St Thomas More Group

1 Come, light of the world,
light up our lives, Lord;
come, light of the world,
light up our hearts.
Dispel all our darkness,
remove all our blindness;
come, light of the world,
be light for our eyes.

2 Come, strength of our days,
strengthen our lives, Lord;
come, strength of our days,
strengthen our hearts.
Come fill us with courage,
to follow you always;
come, strength of our days,
be strength for our minds.

3 Come, joy for the world,
fill us with gladness;
come, joy for the world,
gladden our hearts.
Come bring us together,
with singing and laughter;
come, joy for the world,
bring warmth to our lives.

4 Come, hope of the world,
comfort your people;
come, hope of the world,
comfort our hearts.
Come heal all our sorrow
with love and compassion;
come, hope of the world
bring peace to us all.

5 Come, Spirit of God,
be with us now, Lord;
come, Spirit of God,
fill us with truth.
Enlighten our lives, Lord,
with radiance and power;
come, Spirit of God,
inspire all we do.

65
Henry Alford
© in this version Jubilate Hymns

1 Come, you thankful people, come,
  raise the song of harvest home!
  fruit and crops are gathered in
  safe before the storms begin:
  God our maker will provide
  for our needs to be supplied;
  come, with all his people, come,
  raise the song of harvest home!

2 All the world is God's own field,
  harvests for his praise to yield;
  wheat and weeds together sown
  here for joy or sorrow grown:
  first the blade and then the ear,
  then the full corn shall appear –
  Lord of harvest, grant that we
  wholesome grain and pure may be.

3 For the Lord our God shall come
  and shall bring his harvest home;
  he himself on that great day,
  worthless things shall take away,
  give his angels charge at last
  in the fire the weeds to cast,
  but the fruitful ears to store
  in his care for evermore.

4 Even so, Lord, quickly come –
  bring your final harvest home!
  gather all your people in
  free from sorrow, free from sin,
  there together purified,
  ever thankful at your side –
  come, with all your angels, come,
  bring that glorious harvest home!

66
From John 20
© Michael Perry / Jubilate Hymns

1 Comes Mary to the grave:
  no singing bird has spoken,
  nor has the world awoken,
  and in her grief all love lies lost and broken.

2 Says Jesus at her side,
  no longer Jesus dying,
  'Why Mary, are you crying?'
  She turns, with joy,
      'My Lord! my love!' replying.

3 With Mary on this day
  we join our voices praising
  the God of Jesus' raising,
  and sing the triumph of his love amazing.

67
Donald Hughes
© Methodist Publishing House

1 Creator of the earth and skies,
  to whom all truth and power belong:
  grant us your truth to make us wise,
  grant us your power to make us strong.

2 We have not known you: to the skies
  our monuments of folly soar;
  and all our self-wrought miseries
  have made us trust ourselves the more.

3 We have not loved you: far and wide
  the wreckage of our hatred spreads;
  and evils wrought by human pride
  recoil on unrepentant heads.

4 We long to end this worldwide strife:
  how shall we follow in your way?
  Speak to us all your words of life
  until our darkness turns to day!

68
After Rabanus Maurus and John Cosin
© in this version Jubilate Hymns

1 Creator Spirit, come, inspire
  our lives with light and heavenly fire;
  now make us willing to receive
  the sevenfold gifts you freely give.

2 Your pure anointing from above
  is comfort, life, and fire of love:
  so heal with your eternal light
  the blindness of our human sight.

3 Anoint and cheer our saddened face
  with all the fulness of your grace;
  remove our fears, give peace at home –
  where you are guide, no harm can come.

4 Teach us to know the Father, Son,
  and you with them the Three-in-One;
  whose praise through all the ages long
  shall be our theme, our endless song!

69
Matthew Bridges and Godfrey Thring
© in this version Jubilate Hymns

1 Crown him with many crowns,
  the Lamb upon his throne,
  while heaven's eternal anthem drowns
  all music but its own!
  Awake, my soul, and sing
  of him who died to be
  your saviour and your matchless king
  through all eternity.

2 Crown him the Lord of life
triumphant from the grave,
who rose victorious from the strife
for those he came to save:
his glories now we sing
who died and reigns on high;
who died eternal life to bring
and lives that death may die.

3 Crown him the Lord of love,
who shows his hands and side –
those wounds yet visible above
in beauty glorified.
No angel in the sky
can fully bear the sight,
but downward bends his burning eye
at mysteries so bright.

4 Crown him the Lord of peace –
his kingdom is at hand;
from pole to pole let warfare cease
and Christ rule every land!
A city stands on high,
his glory it displays,
and there the nations 'Holy' cry
in joyful hymns of praise.

5 Crown him the Lord of years,
the potentate of time,
creator of the rolling spheres
in majesty sublime:
all hail, Redeemer, hail,
for you have died for me;
your praise shall never, never fail
through all eternity!

Verse 4 may be omitted

70 Graham Kendrick
© 1985 Thankyou Music

1 Darkness like a shroud
covers the earth,
evil like a cloud
covers the people;
but the Lord will rise upon you,
and his glory will appear on you,
nations will come to your light.
    Arise, shine, your light has come,
    the glory of the Lord has risen on you;
    arise, shine, your light has come –
    Jesus the light of the world has come.

2 Children of the light,
be clean and pure;
rise, you sleepers,
Christ will shine on you:
take the Spirit's flashing two-edged sword
and with faith declare God's mighty word;
stand up, and in his strength be strong!
    Arise, shine . . .

3 Here among us now,
Christ the Light
kindles brighter flames
in our trembling hearts:
Living Word, our lamp, come guide our feet –
as we walk as one in light and peace,
till justice and truth shine like the sun.
    Arise, shine . . .

4 Like a city bright,
so let us blaze;
lights in every street
turning night into day:
and the darkness shall not overcome,
till the fulness of Christ's kingdom comes,
dawning to God's eternal day.
    Arise shine, your light has come,
    the glory of the Lord has risen on you;
    arise, shine, your light has come –
Jesus the light of the world,
Jesus the light of the world,
Jesus the light of the world has come.

A   Your light has come!
B   Your light has come!
A   Your light has come!
B   Your light has come!
ALL Your light has come!

The congregation may divide at A and B

71 John Whittier
© in this version Jubilate Hymns

1 Dear Lord and Father of mankind,
forgive our foolish ways:
reclothe us in our rightful mind;
in purer lives your service find,
    in deeper reverence praise,
    in deeper reverence praise.

2 In simple trust like theirs who heard,
beside the Syrian sea,
the gracious calling of the Lord –
let us, like them, obey his word:
    'Rise up and follow me,
    rise up and follow me!'

3 O sabbath rest by Galilee!
O calm of hills above,
when Jesus shared on bended kneee
the silence of eternity
interpreted by love,
interpreted by love!

4 With that deep hush subduing all
our words and works that drown
the tender whisper of your call,
as noiseless let your blessing fall
as fell your manna down,
as fell your manna down.

5 Drop your still dews of quietness,
till all our strivings cease;
take from our souls the strain and stress,
and let our ordered lives confess
the beauty of your peace,
the beauty of your peace.

6 Breathe through the heats of our desire
your coolness and your balm;
let sense be dumb, let flesh retire,
speak through the earthquake, wind, and fire,
O still small voice of calm,
O still small voice of calm!

72 After Alcuin
© Christopher Idle / Jubilee Hymns

1 Eternal light, shine in my heart,
eternal hope, lift up my eyes;
eternal power, be my support,
eternal wisdom, make me wise.

2 Eternal life, raise me from death,
eternal brightness, make me see;
eternal Spirit, give me breath,
eternal Saviour, come to me:

3 Until by your most costly grace,
invited by your holy word,
at last I come before your face
to know you, my eternal God.

73 From *The Lord's Prayer*, James Seddon
© Mrs M Seddon / Jubilee Hymns

1 Father God in heaven, Lord most high:
hear your children's prayer, Lord most high:
hallowed be your name, Lord most high –
O Lord, hear our prayer.

2 May your kingdom come here on earth;
may your will be done here on earth,
as it is in heaven so on earth –
O Lord, hear our prayer.

3 Give us daily bread day by day,
and forgive our sins day by day,
as we too forgive day by day –
O Lord, hear our prayer.

4 Lead us in your way, make us strong;
when temptations come make us strong;
save us from all sin, keep us strong –
O Lord, hear our prayer.

5 All things come from you, all are yours –
kingdom, glory, power, all are yours;
take our lives and gifts, all are yours –
O Lord, hear our prayer.

74 Daniel Niles
© Christian Conference of Asia

1 Father in heaven,
grant to your children
mercy and blessing,
songs never ceasing;
love to unite us,
grace to redeem us,
Father in heaven,
Father, our God.

2 Jesus redeemer,
may we remember
your gracious passion,
your resurrection:
worship we bring you,
praise we shall sing you,
Jesus redeemer,
Jesus, our Lord.

3 Spirit descending,
whose is the blessing,
strength for the weary,
help for the needy:
sealing Christ's Lordship,
blessing our worship,
Spirit descending,
Spirit adored.

75 John Monsell

1 Fight the good fight with all your might,
Christ is your strength, and Christ your right;
lay hold on life, and it shall be
your joy and crown eternally.

2 Run the straight race
through God's good grace,
lift up your eyes, and seek his face:
life with its way before you lies,
Christ is the path and Christ the prize.

3 Cast care aside, lean on your guide,
   his boundless mercy will provide;
   trust, and your trusting soul shall prove
   Christ is its life, and Christ its love.

4 Faint not, nor fear, his arms are near;
   he does not change, and you are dear;
   only believe and Christ shall be
   your all-in-all eternally.

76 Horatius Bonar

1 Fill now my life, O Lord my God,
   in every part with praise:
   that my whole being may proclaim
   your being and your ways.

2 Not for the lip of praise alone,
   nor yet the praising heart,
   I ask, but for a life made up
   of praise in every part:

3 Praise in the common things of life,
   its goings out and in;
   praise in each duty and each deed,
   exalted or unseen.

4 Fill every part of me with praise;
   let all my being speak
   of you and of your love, O Lord,
   poor though I be and weak.

5 Then, Lord, from me you shall receive
   the praise and glory due;
   and so shall I begin on earth
   the song for ever new.

6 So shall no part of day or night
   from sacredness be free;
   but all my life, with you my God,
   in fellowship shall be.

77 From Psalm 147
© Timothy Dudley-Smith

1 Fill your hearts with joy and gladness,
   sing and praise your God and mine!
   Great the Lord in love and wisdom,
   might and majesty divine!
   He who framed the starry heavens
   knows and names them as they shine.

2 Praise the Lord, his people, praise him!
   wounded souls his comfort know;
   those who fear him find his mercies,
   peace for pain and joy for woe;
   humble hearts are high exalted,
   human pride and power laid low.

3 Praise the Lord for times and seasons,
   cloud and sunshine, wind and rain;
   spring to melt the snows of winter
   till the waters flow again;
   grass upon the mountain pastures,
   golden valleys thick with grain.

4 Fill your hearts with joy and gladness,
   peace and plenty crown your days;
   love his laws, declare his judgements,
   walk in all his words and ways;
   he the Lord and we his children –
   praise the Lord, all people, praise!

78 From John 3, 2 Corinthians 8 and Philippians 2
© Word & Music / Jubilate Hymns

For God so loved the world
   he gave his only Son,
who came to die
   that we might ever live;
and on a cruel cross
   our full redemption won,
that we might know
   the peace he longs to give:
though he was rich,
   he came alone and poor for us;
though he was Lord,
   he served as if a slave;
though he was God,
   our human shape he bore for us;
to earth he came in love,
   his own to seek and save.

Yes, God so loved . . .

79 F Sandford Pierpoint

1 For the beauty of the earth,
   for the beauty of the skies,
   for the love which from our birth
   over and around us lies,
      Christ our God, to you we raise
      this our sacrifice of praise.

2 For the beauty of each hour
   of the day and of the night,
   hill and vale, and tree and flower,
   sun and moon and stars of light,
      Christ our God . . .

3 For the joy of ear and eye,
   for the heart and mind's delight,
   for the mystic harmony
   linking sense to sound and sight,
      Christ our God . . .

4 For the joy of human love,
brother, sister, parent, child,
friends on earth and friends above,
pleasures pure and undefiled,
    Christ our God . . .

5 For each perfect gift divine
to our race so freely given,
joys bestowed by love's design,
flowers of earth and fruits of heaven,
    Christ our God . . .

80 Louis Benson

1 For the bread which you have broken,
for the wine which you have poured,
for the words which you have spoken,
now we give you thanks, O Lord.

2 By these pledges that you love us,
by your gift of peace restored,
by your call to heaven above us,
consecrate our lives, O Lord:

3 In your service, Lord, defend us,
help us to obey your word;
in the world to which you send us
let your kingdom come, O Lord!

81 From Psalm 130
© David Preston / Jubilate Hymns

1 From deep despair to you I call:
Lord, hear me when I cry!
O turn your ear to hear my voice
which pleads with you on high!

2 O Lord, if you record our sins,
who ever could be spared?
But mercy may be found with you,
that you may then be feared.

3 Now for the Lord my spirit waits,
my hope is in his word;
more than the watchmen wait for dawn
my soul waits for the Lord.

4 O Israel, hope in God the Lord!
His grace is full and free,
and pays the price to ransom us
from all iniquity.

82 Frederick Pratt Green
© Stainer & Bell Ltd

1 For the fruits of his creation,
    thanks be to God;
for his gifts to every nation,
    thanks be to God;
for the ploughing, sowing, reaping,
silent growth while we are sleeping,
future needs in earth's safe-keeping,
    thanks be to God.

2 In the just reward of labour,
    God's will is done;
in the help we give our neighbour,
    God's will is done;
in our worldwide task of caring
for the hungry and despairing,
in the harvests we are sharing,
    God's will is done.

3 For the harvests of the Spirit,
    thanks be to God;
for the good we all inherit,
    thanks be to God;
for the wonders that astound us,
for the truths that still confound us,
most of all, that love has found us,
    thanks be to God.

83 Rosamund Herklots
© Oxford University Press

1 'Forgive our sins as we forgive,'
you taught us, Lord, to pray;
but you alone can grant us grace
to live the words we say.

2 How can your pardon reach and bless
the unforgiving heart
that broods on wrongs, and will not let
old bitterness depart?

3 In blazing light your cross reveals
the truth we dimly knew:
what trivial debts are owed to us,
how great our debt to you!

4 Lord, cleanse the depths within our souls
and bid resentment cease;
then, bound to all in bonds of love,
our lives will spread your peace.

84 © Christopher Idle / Jubilate Hymns

1 Freedom and life are ours
    for Christ has set us free!
  Never again submit to powers
    that lead to slavery:
  Christ is the Lord who breaks
    our chains, our bondage ends,
  Christ is the rescuer who makes
    the helpless slaves his friends.

2 Called by the Lord to use
    our freedom and be strong,
  not letting liberty excuse
    a life of blatant wrong:
  freed from the law's stern hand
    God's gift of grace to prove,
  know that the law's entire demand
    is gladly met by love.

3 Spirit of God, come, fill,
    emancipate us all!
  Speak to us, Word of truth, until
    before his throne we fall:
  glory and liberty
    our Father has decreed,
  and if the Son shall make us free
    we shall be free indeed!

85 Graham Kendrick
    © 1983 Thankyou Music

1 From heaven you came, helpless Babe –
    entered our world your glory veiled,
  not to be served but to serve,
  and give your life that we might live.
      This is our God – the servant king,
      he calls us now to follow him,
      to bring our lives as a daily offering
      of worship to the servant king.

2 There in the garden of tears
  my heavy load he chose to bear;
  his heart with sorrow was torn,
  'Yet not my will but yours,' he said.
      This is our God . . .

3 Come see his hands and his feet,
  the scars that speak of sacrifice;
  hands that flung stars into space
  to cruel nails surrendered.
      This is our God . . .

4 So let us learn how to serve
  and in our lives enthrone him,
  each other's needs to prefer –
  for it is Christ we are serving.
      This is our God . . .

86 Graham Kendrick
    © 1988 Make Way Music

1 From the sun's rising unto the sun's setting
  Jesus our Lord shall be great in the earth;
  and all earth's kingdom
      shall be his dominion –
  all of creation shall sing of his worth.
      Let every heart, every voice,
      every tongue join with spirits ablaze:
      one in his love
      we will circle the world
      with the song of his praise.
      O let all his people rejoice,
      and let all the earth hear his voice!

2 To every tongue, tribe
      and nation he sends us,
  to make disciples to teach and baptize;
  for all authority to him is given –
  now as his witnesses we shall arise.
      Let every heart . . .

3 Come let us join with
      the church from all nations,
  cross every border, throw wide every door:
  workers with him as he gathers his harvest,
  till earth's far corners our saviour adore.
      Let every heart . . .

      Let all his people rejoice,
      and let all the earth hear his voice!

87 © Michael Perry / Jubilate Hymns

1 Glad music fills the Christmas sky –
  a hymn of praise, a song of love;
  the angels worship high above
  and Mary sings her lullaby.

2 Of tender love for God she sings,
  the chosen mother of the Son;
  she knows that wonders have begun,
  and trusts for all the future brings.

3 The angel chorus of the skies
  who come to tell us of God's grace
  have yet to know his human face,
  to watch him die, to see him rise.

4 Let praise be true and love sincere,
  rejoice to greet the saviour's birth;
  let peace and honour fill the earth
  and mercy reign – for God is here!

5 Then lift your hearts and voices high,
  sing once again the Christmas song:
  for love and praise to Christ belong –
  in shouts of joy, and lullaby.

88   From the Italian
          Edward Caswall

1   Glory be to Jesus,
    who, in bitter pains,
    poured for me the life-blood
    from his sacred veins.

2   Grace and life eternal
    in that blood I find:
    blessed be his compassion
    wonderfully kind!

3   Abel's blood for vengeance
    pleaded to the skies,
    but the blood of Jesus
    for our pardon cries.

4   When that blood is sprinkled
    on our guilty hearts,
    Satan in confusion
    terror-struck departs.

5   When this earth exulting
    lifts its praise on high,
    angel hosts rejoicing
    make their glad reply.

6   Raise your thankful voices,
    swell the mighty flood;
    louder still and louder
    praise the Lamb of God!

Tune: Land of hope & glory

89   From 'Gloria in excelsis'
          © Christopher Idle / Jubilate Hymns

1   Glory in the highest
        to the God of heaven!
    Peace to all your people
        through the earth be given!
    Mighty God and Father,
        thanks and praise we bring,
    singing Hallelujah
        to our heavenly king;
    singing Hallelujah
        to our heavenly king.

2   Jesus Christ is risen,
        God the Father's Son!
    With the Holy Spirit,
        you are Lord alone!
    Lamb once killed for sinners,
        all our guilt to bear,
    show us now your mercy,
        now receive our prayer;
    show us now your mercy,
        now receive our prayer.

3   Christ the world's true Saviour,
        high and holy one,
    seated now and reigning
        from your Father's throne:
    Lord and God, we praise you!
        Highest heaven adores:
    in the Father's glory,
        all the praise be yours;
    in the Father's glory,
        all the praise be yours!

90   James Seddon
          © Mrs M Seddon / Jubilate Hymns

1   Go forth and tell! O church of God, awake!
    God's saving news to all the nations take;
    proclaim Christ Jesus,
        saviour, Lord and king,
    that all the world his worthy praise may sing.

2   Go forth and tell! God's love embraces all;
    he will in grace respond to all who call:
    how shall they call if they have never heard
    the gracious invitation of his word?

3   Go forth and tell where still the darkness lies;
    in wealth or want, the sinner surely dies:
    give us, O Lord, concern of heart and mind,
    a love like yours compassionate and kind.

4   Go forth and tell! The doors are open wide:
    share God's good gifts – let no one be denied;
    live out your life
        as Christ your Lord shall choose,
    your ransomed powers for his sole glory use.

5   Go forth and tell! O church of God, arise!
    go in the strength which Christ your Lord
        supplies;
    go till all nations his great name adore
    and serve him, Lord and king for evermore.

91   After R Pynson

    God be in my head
    and in my understanding.

    God be in my eyes
    and in my looking.

    God be in my mouth
    and in my speaking.

    God be in my heart
    and in my thinking.

    God be at my end
    and at my departing.

92
From Isaiah 12
© Christopher Idle / Jubilate Hymns

1 God brings us comfort
       where his anger burned,
so judgement and fear
       to peace and trust are turned.
    Praise God today:
    his mercies never end;
    our judge becomes in Christ
    our greatest friend,
    our judge becomes our greatest friend.

2 Wells of salvation streams of life will bring;
with joy we shall draw
       from this refreshing spring.
    Praise God today:
    his blessings never end;
    our judge becomes in Christ
    our greatest friend,
    our judge becomes our greatest friend.

3 Songs shall be his for this victorious day:
give thanks to his name,
       and teach the earth to say,
    Praise God today:
    his triumphs never end;
    our judge becomes in Christ
    our greatest friend,
    our judge becomes our greatest friend.

4 Love lives among us, Israel's holy One
who comes to the rescue –
       see what God has done!
    Praise God today:
    his wonders never end;
    our judge becomes in Christ
    our greatest friend,
    our judge becomes our greatest friend.

93
Percy Dearmer

1 God is love – his the care,
tending each, everywhere;
God is love – all is there!
Jesus came to show him,
that we all might know him.
    Sing aloud, loud, loud;
    sing aloud, loud, loud:
    God is good,
    God is truth, God is beauty – praise him!

2 Jesus shared all our pain,
lived and died, rose again,
rules our hearts, now as then –
for he came to save us
by the truth he gave us.
    Sing aloud . . .

3 To our Lord praise we sing –
light and life, friend and king,
coming down love to bring,
pattern for our duty,
showing God in beauty.
    Sing aloud . . .

94
George Briggs
© 1953, 1981 The Hymn Society,
Texas Christian University

1 God has spoken – by his prophets,
spoken his unchanging word;
each from age to age proclaiming
God the one, the righteous Lord;
in the world's despair and turmoil
one firm anchor still holds fast:
God is king, his throne eternal,
God the first and God the last.

2 God has spoken – by Christ Jesus,
Christ, the everlasting Son;
brightness of the Father's glory,
with the Father ever one:
spoken by the Word incarnate,
Life, before all time began,
light of light, to earth descending,
God, revealed as Son of Man.

3 God is speaking – by his Spirit
speaking to our hearts again;
in the age-long word expounding
God's own message, now as then.
Through the rise and fall of nations
one sure faith is standing fast:
God abides, his word unchanging,
God the first and God the last.

95
From Psalm 46
© Richard Bewes / Jubilate Hymns

1 God is our strength and refuge,
our present help in trouble;
and we therefore will not fear,
though the earth should change!
Though mountains shake and tremble,
though swirling floods are raging,
God the Lord of hosts is with us evermore!

2 There is a flowing river
within God's holy city;
God is in the midst of her –
she shall not be moved!
God's help is swiftly given,
thrones vanish at his presence –
God the Lord of hosts is with us evermore!

3 Come, see the works of our maker,
   learn of his deeds all-powerful:
   wars will cease across the world
   when he shatters the spear!
   Be still and know your creator,
   uplift him in the nations –
   God the Lord of hosts is with us evermore!

1 God is our fortress and our rock,
   our mighty help in danger;
   he shields us from the battle's shock
   and thwarts the devil's anger:
      for still the prince of night
      prolongs his evil fight;
      he uses every skill
      to work his wicked will –
      no earthly force is like him.

2 Our hope is fixed on Christ alone,
   the Man, of God's own choosing;
   without him nothing can be won
   and fighting must be losing:
      so let the powers accursed
      come on and do their worst,
      the Son of God shall ride
      to battle at our side,
      and he shall have the victory.

3 The word of God will not be slow
   while demon hordes surround us,
   though evil strike its cruellest blow
   and death and hell confound us:
      for even if distress
      should take all we possess,
      and those who mean us ill
      should ravage, wreck, or kill,
      God's kingdom is immortal!

1 God of mercy, God of grace,
      show the brightness of your face;
   shine upon us, Saviour shine,
      fill your church with light divine,
   and your saving health extend
      to the earth's remotest end.

2 Let the people praise you, Lord!
      Be by all who live adored;
   let the nations shout and sing
      glory to their saviour king,
   at your feet their tribute pay,
      and your holy will obey.

3 Let the people crown you king!
      Then shall earth her harvest bring,
   God to us his blessing give,
      we to God devoted live;
   all below and all above,
      one in joy and light and love.

1 God of gods, we sound his praises,
   highest heaven its homage brings;
   earth and all creation raises
   glory to the King of kings:
   holy, holy, holy, name him,
   Lord of all his hosts proclaim him;
   to the everlasting Father
   every tongue in triumph sings.

2 Christians in their hearts enthrone him,
   tell his praises wide abroad;
   prophets, priests, apostles own him
   martyrs' crown and saints' reward.
   Three-in-One his glory sharing,
   earth and heaven his praise declaring,
   praise the high majestic Father,
   praise the everlasting Lord!

3 Hail the Christ, the King of glory,
   he whose praise the angels cry;
   born to share our human story,
   love and labour, grieve and die:
   by his cross his work completed,
   sinners ransomed, death defeated;
   in the glory of the Father
   Christ ascended reigns on high.

4 Lord, we look for your returning;
   teach us so to walk your ways,
   hearts and minds your will discerning,
   lives alight with joy and praise:
   in your love and care enfold us,
   by your constancy uphold us,
   may your mercy, Lord and Father,
   keep us now and all our days!

1 God rest you merry, gentlemen,
   let nothing you dismay!
   for Jesus Christ our saviour
   was born on Christmas Day,
   to save us all from Satan's power
   when we were gone astray:
      O tidings of comfort and joy,
      comfort and joy!
      O tidings of comfort and joy!

2 At Bethlehem in Judah
the holy babe was born;
they laid him in a manger
on this most happy morn:
at which his mother Mary
did neither fear nor scorn:
  O tidings of comfort and joy,
  comfort and joy!
  O tidings of comfort and joy!

3 From God our heavenly Father
a holy angel came;
the shepherds saw the glory
and heard the voice proclaim
that Christ was born in Bethlehem –
and Jesus is his name:
  O tidings of comfort and joy . . .

4 Fear not, then said the angel,
let nothing cause you fright;
to you is born a saviour
in David's town tonight,
to free all those who trust in him
from Satan's power and might:
  O tidings of comfort and joy . . .

5 The shepherds at these tidings
rejoiced in heart and mind,
and on the darkened hillside
they left their flocks behind,
and went to Bethlehem straightway
this holy child to find:
  O tidings of comfort and joy . . .

6 And when to Bethlehem they came
where Christ the infant lay:
they found him in a manger
where oxen fed on hay,
and there beside her newborn child
his mother knelt to pray:
  O tidings of comfort and joy . . .

7 Now to the Lord sing praises,
all people in this place!
With Christian love and fellowship
each other now embrace,
and let this Christmas festival
all bitterness displace:
  O tidings of comfort and joy . . .

Either verses 2 and 6 or verses 4 and 5 may be omitted

100   John Marriott

1 God, whose almighty word
chaos and darkness heard,
and took their flight:
hear us, we humbly pray,
and where the gospel-day
sheds not its glorious ray,
  let there be light!

2 Saviour, who came to bring
on your redeeming wing
healing and sight,
health to the sick in mind,
sight to the inly blind:
O now to all mankind
  let there be light!

3 Spirit of truth and love –
life-giving, holy dove,
speed on your flight!
move on the water's face
bearing the lamp of grace
and, in earth's darkest place,
  let there be light!

4 Gracious and holy Three,
glorious Trinity,
wisdom, love, might:
boundless as ocean's tide
rolling in fullest pride
through the world far and wide,
  let there be light!

101   After St Boniface
© Michael Perry / Jubilate Hymns

1 God whose love we cannot measure,
  hear our song of thanks, we pray.
Who could ever count the blessings
  that surround us every day?
For you give us light in darkness,
  in our weakness make us strong;
by your peace and tender comfort
  turn our sorrow into song.

2 In our hearts we bless and praise you –
  you have borne our heavy load;
here we thank you for your goodness –
  we your people, you our God:
Father, Son and Holy Spirit,
  Lord whose name we lift above,
you are Love from everlasting
  and to everlasting Love!

102   From In dulci jubilo
John Neale

1 Good Christians all, rejoice
with heart and soul and voice!
Listen now to what we say,
Jesus Christ is born today:
ox and ass before him bow
and he is in the manger now!
  Christ is born today;
  Christ is born today!

2 Good Christians all, rejoice
with heart and soul and voice!
Hear the news of endless bliss,
Jesus Christ was born for this:
he has opened heaven's door
and we are blessed for evermore!
    Christ was born for this;
    Christ was born for this.

3 Good Christians all, rejoice
with heart and soul and voice!
Now you need not fear the grave,
Jesus Christ was born to save:
come at his most gracious call
to find salvation, one and all!
    Christ was born to save;
    Christ was born to save!

103
Thomas Chisholm
in this version Jubilate Hymns
© 1923 and 1951 Hope Publishing Company

1 Great is your faithfulness, O God my Father,
you have fulfilled all your promise to me;
you never fail and your love is unchanging –
all you have been, you for ever will be.
    Great is your faithfulness,
    great is your faithfulness,
    morning by morning new mercies I see;
    all I have needed your hand has provided –
    great is your faithfulness, Father, to me.

2 Summer and winter,
    and springtime and harvest,
sun, moon and stars in their courses above
join with all nature in eloquent witness
to your great faithfulness, mercy and love.
    Great is your faithfulness . . .

3 Pardon for sin, and a peace everlasting,
your living presence to cheer and to guide;
strength for today,
    and bright hope for tomorrow –
these are the blessings your love will provide.
    Great is your faithfulness . . .

104
Peter Williams and others

1 Guide me, O my great Redeemer,
pilgrim through this barren land:
I am weak, but you are mighty –
hold me with your powerful hand:
    Bread of heaven, Bread of heaven,
    feed me now and evermore;
    feed me now and evermore!

2 Open now the crystal fountain
where the healing waters flow;
let the fiery, cloudy pillar
lead me all my journey through:
    Strong Deliverer, strong Deliverer,
    ever be my strength and shield;
    ever be my strength and shield.

3 When I tread the verge of Jordan
bid my anxious fears subside;
Death of death, and hell's Destruction,
land me safe on Canaan's side:
    Songs of praises, songs of praises,
    all my joy shall ever be;
    all my joy shall ever be.

105
© Timothy Dudley-Smith

1 Had he not loved us
he had never come,
yet is he love
and love is all his way;
low to the mystery
of the virgin's womb
Christ bows his glory –
born on Christmas Day.

2 Had he not loved us
he had never come;
had he not come
he need have never died,
nor won the victory
of the vacant tomb,
the awful triumph
of the Crucified.

3 Had he not loved us
he had never come;
still were we lost
in sorrow, sin and shame,
the doors fast shut
on our eternal home
which now stand open –
for he loved and came.

106
Charles Wesley and Thomas Cotterill

1 Hail the day that sees him rise
    Alleluia,
to his throne beyond the skies:
    alleluia,
Christ, the Lamb for sinners given,
    alleluia,
enters now the highest heaven:
    alleluia!

2 There for him high triumph waits:
 Alleluia,
lift your heads, eternal gates –
 alleluia,
he has conquered death and sin,
 alleluia,
take the King of glory in:
 alleluia!

3 See! the heaven its Lord receives,
 Alleluia,
yet he loves the earth he leaves;
 alleluia,
though returning to his throne,
 alleluia,
still he calls mankind his own.
 alleluia!

4 Still for us he intercedes,
 Alleluia,
his prevailing death he pleads,
 alleluia,
near himself prepares our place,
 alleluia,
he the first-fruits of our race.
 alleluia!

5 Lord, though parted from our sight
 Alleluia,
far beyond the starry height,
 alleluia,
lift our hearts that we may rise
 alleluia,
one with you beyond the skies:
 alleluia!

6 There with you we shall remain,
 Alleluia,
share the glory of your reign;
 alleluia,
there your face unclouded view,
 alleluia,
find our heaven of heavens in you.
 alleluia!

107   James Montgomery

1 Hail to the Lord's anointed,
great David's greater son!
Hail, in the time appointed
his reign on earth begun!
He comes to break oppression,
to set the captive free,
to take away transgression
and rule in equity.

2 He comes with comfort speedy
to those who suffer wrong,
to save the poor and needy
and help the weak be strong;
to give them songs for sighing,
their darkness turn to light,
whose souls, condemned and dying,
are precious in his sight.

3 He shall come down like showers
upon the fruitful earth,
and love, joy, hope, like flowers
spring in his path to birth;
before him on the mountains
shall peace, the herald, go,
and righteousness in fountains
from hill to valley flow.

4 Kings shall bow down before him
and gold and incense bring,
all nations shall adore him,
his praise all people sing;
to him shall prayer unceasing
and daily vows ascend;
his kingdom still increasing,
a kingdom without end.

108   Charles Wesley and others

1 Hark! the herald angels sing
glory to the new-born King;
peace on earth and mercy mild,
God and sinners reconciled!
Joyful all you nations rise,
join the triumph of the skies;
with the angelic host proclaim,
'Christ is born in Bethlehem'.
 Hark! the herald angels sing
 glory to the new-born King.

2 Christ, by highest heaven adored,
Christ, the everlasting Lord:
late in time behold him come,
offspring of a virgin's womb;
veiled in flesh the Godhead see,
hail the incarnate Deity!
pleased as man with us to dwell,
Jesus our Emmanuel:
 Hark! the herald . . .

3 Hail the heaven-born Prince of peace,
hail the Sun of righteousness:
light and life to all he brings,
risen with healing in his wings;
mild, he lays his glory by,
born that we no more may die,
born to raise us from the earth,
born to give us second birth.
 Hark! the herald . . .

109

1 He gave his life in selfless love,
    for sinners once he came;
he had no stain of sin himself
    but bore our guilt and shame:
he took the cup of pain and death,
    his blood was freely shed;
we see his body on the cross,
    we share the living bread.

2 He did not come to call the good
    but sinners to repent;
it was the lame, the deaf, the blind
    for whom his life was spent:
to heal the sick, to find the lost –
    it was for such he came,
and round his table all may come
    to praise his holy name.

3 They heard him call his Father's name –
    then 'Finished!' was his cry;
like them we have forsaken him
    and left him there to die:
the sins that crucified him then
    are sins his blood has cured;
the love that bound him to a cross
    our freedom has ensured.

4 His body broken once for us
    is glorious now above;
the cup of blessing we receive,
    a sharing of his love:
as in his presence we partake,
    his dying we proclaim
until the hour of majesty
    when Jesus comes again.

110

1 He healed the darkness of my mind
the day he gave my sight to me:
it was not sin that made me blind:
it was no sinner made me see,
it was no sinner made me see.

2 Let others call my faith a lie,
or try to stir up doubt in me:
look at me now! None can deny
I once was blind and now I see!
I once was blind and now I see!

3 Ask me not how! But I know who
has opened up new worlds to me:
this Jesus does what none can do
I once was blind and now I see.
I once was blind and now I see.

111

1 He lives in us, the Christ of God,
    his Spirit joins with ours;
he brings to us the Father's grace
    with powers beyond our powers.
And if enticing sin grows strong,
    when human nature fails,
God's Spirit in our inner self
    fights with us, and prevails.

2 Our pangs of guilt and fears of death
    are Satan's stratagems –
by Jesus Christ who died for us
    God pardons: who condemns?
And when we cannot feel our faith,
    nor bring ourselves to pray,
the Spirit pleads with God for us
    in words we could not say.

3 God gave the Son to save us all –
    no greater love is known!
And shall that love abandon us
    who have become Christ's own?
For God has raised him from the grave,
    in this we stand assured;
so none can tear us from the love
    of Jesus Christ our Lord.

112

1 He stood before the court
on trial instead of us;
he met its power to hurt,
condemned to face the cross:
our king, accused
of treachery;
our God, abused
for blasphemy!

2 These are the crimes that tell
the tale of human guilt;
our sins, our death, our hell –
on these the case is built:
to this world's powers
their Lord stays dumb;
the guilt is ours,
no answers come.

3 The sentence must be passed,
the unknown prisoner killed;
the price is paid at last,
the law of God fulfilled:
he takes our blame,
and from that day
the accuser's claim
is wiped away.

4 Shall we be judged and tried?
In Christ our trial is done;
we live, for he has died,
our condemnation gone:
in Christ are we
both dead and raised,
alive and free –
his name be praised!

113 © Michael Perry / Jubilate Hymns

1 Heal me, hands of Jesus,
and search out all my pain;
restore my hope, remove my fear
and bring me peace again.

2 Cleanse me, blood of Jesus,
take bitterness away;
let me forgive as one forgiven
and bring me peace today.

3 Know me, mind of Jesus,
and show me all my sin;
dispel the memories of guilt
and bring me peace within.

4 Fill me, joy of Jesus:
anxiety shall cease
and heaven's serenity be mine,
for Jesus brings me peace!

114 Maggi Dawn
© 1987 Thankyou Music

1 He was pierced for our transgressions,
and bruised for our iniquities;
and to bring us peace he was punished,
and by his stripes we are healed.

2 He was led like a lamb to the slaughter,
although he was innocent of crime;
and cut off from the land of the living,
he paid for the guilt that was mine.

We like sheep have gone astray,
turned each one to our own way,
and the Lord has laid on him
the iniquity of us all.
We like sheep . . .

DESCANT
Like a lamb,
to the slaughter he came.
And the Lord laid on him
the iniquity of us all.

115 © Michael Saward / Jubilate Hymns

1 He who created light
from his commanding height,
his voice was heard.
Then through sea, sky and earth,
labouring, came to birth,
sign of eternal worth,
life through God's word.

2 He who was born to save,
standing at Lazarus' grave,
his voice was heard.
He who had healed the lame,
called to the dead by name,
and from the tomb there came
life through God's word.

3 He whose inspiring power
surges through every hour,
his voice is heard.
Strong as the wind he blows,
swift as a torrent flows,
and to the church bestows
life through God's word.

4 He who is three-in-one,
God – Father, Spirit, Son –
his voice is heard.
To him our hearts we raise,
singing our hymns of praise,
sharing, in all our ways,
life through God's word.

116 From Psalm 86
© Michael Perry / Jubilate Hymns

1 Hear me, O Lord, and respond to my prayer,
guard well my life, for I love you:
nothing compares with the wonders you do,
for there is no god above you.

2 Bring me your joy as I worship you, Lord,
come to my heart, for I need you;
teach me your way,
let me walk in your truth –
I cannot fail when I heed you.

3 Give me a sign of your goodness, O Lord,
grant me the strength that obeys you:
you are compassion, abounding in love,
you are my king, and I praise you!

117
From Revelation 4, 5
© Timothy Dudley-Smith

1 Heavenly hosts in ceaseless worship
'Holy, holy, holy!' cry;
'He who is, who was and will be,
God almighty, Lord most high.'
Praise and honour, power and glory,
be to him who reigns alone!
We, with all his hands have fashioned,
fall before the Father's throne.

2 All creation, all redemption,
join to sing the Saviour's worth;
Lamb of God whose blood has bought us,
kings and priests, to reign on earth.
Wealth and wisdom, power and glory,
honour, might, dominion, praise,
now be his from all his creatures
and to everlasting days!

3 Gone is their thirst
and no more shall they hunger,
God is their shelter, his power at their side;
sun shall not pain them,
no burning will torture,
Jesus the Lamb is their shepherd and guide.

4 He will go with them to clear living water
flowing from springs
which his mercy supplies;
gone is their grief and their trials are over –
God wipes away every tear from their eyes.

5 Blessing and glory and wisdom and power
be to the Saviour again and again;
might and thanksgiving and honour for ever
be to our God: Alleluia! Amen.

118
Charles Wesley
© in this version Jubilate Hymns

1 Help us to help each other, Lord,
each other's load to bear;
that all may live in true accord,
our joys and pains to share.

2 Help us to build each other up,
your strength within us prove;
increase our faith, confirm our hope,
and fill us with your love.

3 Together make us free indeed –
your life within us show;
and into you, our living head,
let us in all things grow.

4 Drawn by the magnet of your love
we find our hearts made new:
nearer each other let us move,
and nearer still to you.

119
From Revelation 7
© Christopher Idle / Jubilate Hymns

1 Here from all nations, all tongues
and all peoples,
countless the crowd but their voices are one;
vast is the sight and majestic their singing –
'God has the victory:
he reigns from the throne!'

2 These have come
out of the hardest oppression,
now they may stand in the presence of God,
serving their Lord day and night
in his temple,
ransomed and cleansed
by the Lamb's precious blood.

120
Horatius Bonar

1 Here, O my Lord, I see you face to face,
here faith can touch and handle
things unseen;
here I will grasp with firmer hand your grace
and all my weariness upon you lean.

2 Here I will feed upon the bread of God,
here drink with you the royal wine of heaven;
here I will lay aside each earthly load,
here taste afresh the calm of sin forgiven.

3 I have no help but yours, nor do I need
another arm but yours to lean upon;
it is enough, my Lord, enough indeed,
my hope is in your strength,
your strength alone.

4 Mine is the sin, but yours the righteousness;
mine is the guilt,
but yours the cleansing blood:
here is my robe, my refuge, and my peace;
your blood, your righteousness,
O Lord my God.

5 Too soon we rise, the symbols disappear;
the feast, though not the love,
is past and done:
gone are the bread and wine,
but you are here,
nearer than ever, still my shield and sun.

6 Feast after feast thus comes and passes by,
yet, passing, points to that glad feast above;
giving sweet foretaste of the festal joy,
the Lamb's great bridal feast of bliss and love.

121

1 Holy child, how still you lie!
safe the manger, soft the hay;
faint upon the eastern sky
breaks the dawn of Christmas Day.

2 Holy child, whose birthday brings
shepherds from their field and fold,
angel choirs and eastern kings,
myrrh and frankincense and gold:

3 Holy child, what gift of grace
from the Father freely willed!
In your infant form we trace
all God's promises fulfilled.

4 Holy child, whose human years
span like ours delight and pain;
one in human joys and tears,
one in all but sin and stain:

5 Holy child, so far from home,
all the lost to seek and save,
to what dreadful death you come,
to what dark and silent grave!

6 Holy child, before whose name
powers of darkness faint and fall;
conquered, death and sin and shame –
Jesus Christ is Lord of all!

7 Holy child, how still you lie!
safe the manger, soft the hay;
clear upon the eastern sky
breaks the dawn of Christmas Day.

122

Reginald Heber

1 Holy, holy, holy, Lord God almighty!
early in the morning
our song of praise shall be:
Holy, holy, holy! – merciful and mighty,
God in three persons, glorious Trinity.

2 Holy, holy, holy! All the saints adore you
casting down their golden crowns
around the glassy sea,
cherubim and seraphim
falling down before you:
you were and are, and evermore shall be!

3 Holy, holy, holy!
Though the darkness hide you,
though the sinful human eye
your glory may not see,
you alone are holy, there is none beside you,
perfect in power, in love and purity.

4 Holy, holy, holy, Lord God almighty!
all your works shall praise your name,
in earth and sky and sea:
Holy, holy, holy! – merciful and mighty,
God in three persons, glorious Trinity.

Traditional version

1 Holy, holy, holy, Lord God almighty!
early in the morning
our song shall rise to thee:
Holy, holy, holy! – merciful and mighty,
God in three persons, blessèd Trinity.

2 Holy, holy, holy! All the saints adore thee,
casting down their golden crowns
around the glassy sea;
cherubim and seraphim
falling down before thee:
God from of old who evermore shall be!

3 Holy, holy, holy! –
though the darkness hide thee,
though the eye of sinful man
thy glory may not see;
only thou art holy, there is none beside thee
perfect in power, in love and purity.

4 Holy, holy, holy, Lord God almighty!
all thy works shall praise thy name,
in earth and sky and sea:
Holy, holy, holy! – merciful and mighty,
God in three persons, blessèd Trinity.

123

1 Holy Spirit, gracious guest,
hear and grant our heart's request
for that gift supreme and best:
holy heavenly love.

2 Faith that mountains could remove,
tongues of earth or heaven above,
knowledge, all things, empty prove
if I have no love.

3 Though I as a martyr bleed,
give my goods the poor to feed,
all is vain if love I need:
therefore give me love.

4 Love is kind and suffers long,
love is pure and thinks no wrong,
love than death itself more strong:
therefore give us love.

5 Prophecy will fade away,
melting in the light of day;
love will ever with us stay:
therefore give us love.

6 Faith and hope and love we see
joining hand in hand agree –
but the greatest of the three,
and the best is love,
the best is love,
the best is love.

124
Brian Foley
© 1971 Faber Music Ltd

1 How can we sing with joy to God,
how can we pray to him,
when we are far away from God
in selfishness and sin?

2 How can we claim to do God's will
when we have turned away
from things of God to things of earth,
and willed to disobey?

3 How can we praise the love of God
which all his works make known,
when all our works turn from his love
to choices of our own?

4 God knows the sinful things we do,
the godless life we live,
yet in his love he calls to us,
so ready to forgive.

5 So we will turn again to God –
his ways will be our ways,
his will our will, his love our love,
and he himself our praise!

125
Richard Keen
© in this version Jubilate Hymns

1 How firm a foundation, you people of God,
is laid for your faith in his excellent word!
What more can he say to you than he has said
to everyone trusting in Jesus our head?

2 Since Jesus is with you, do not be afraid:
since he is your Lord,
you need not be dismayed;
he strengthens you, guards you,
and helps you to stand,
upheld by his righteous, omnipotent hand.

3 When through the deep waters
he calls you to go,
the rivers of trouble shall not overflow;
the Lord will be with you,
to help and to bless,
and work for your good
through your deepest distress.

4 When through fiery trials
your pathway shall lead,
his grace shall sustain you
with all that you need;
the flames shall not hurt you – his only design
your dross to consume
and your gold to refine.

5 Whoever has come to believe in his name
will not be deserted, and not put to shame;
though hell may endeavour
that Christian to shake
his Lord will not leave him, nor ever forsake.

126
Joseph Hart

1 How good is the God we adore!
our faithful, unchangeable friend;
his love is as great as his power
and knows neither measure nor end.

2 For Christ is the first and the last;
his Spirit will guide us safe home:
we'll praise him for all that is past
and trust him for all that's to come.

127
© Christopher Idle / Jubilate Hymns

1 How sure the Scriptures are!
God's vital, urgent word,
as true as steel, and far
more sharp than any sword:
So deep and fine, at his control
they pierce where soul and spirit join.

2 They test each human thought,
refining like a fire;
they measure what we ought
to do and to desire:
For God knows all – exposed it lies
before his eyes to whom we call.

3 Let those who hear his voice
confronting them today,
reject the tempting choice
of doubting or delay:
For God speaks still – his word is clear,
so let us hear and do his will!

128
From Psalm 13
© Barbara Woollett / Jubilate Hymns

1 How long, O Lord,
will you forget
an answer to my prayer?
No tokens of your love I see,
your face is turned away from me:
I wrestle with despair.

2 How long, O Lord,
   will you forsake
   and leave me in this way?
   When will you come to my relief?
   My heart is overwhelmed with grief,
      by evil night and day.

3 How long, O Lord –
   but you forgive,
   with mercy from above.
   I find that all your ways are just,
   I learn to praise you and to trust
      in your unfailing love.

129 John Newton

1 How sweet the name of Jesus sounds
   in a believer's ear!
   It soothes our sorrows, heals our wounds
   and drives away our fear:

2 It makes the wounded spirit whole,
   and calms the troubled breast;
   it satisfies the hungry soul,
   and gives the weary rest,
   (and gives the weary rest.)

3 Dear name – the rock on which I build,
   my shield and hiding-place,
   my never-failing treasury, filled
   with boundless stores of grace!

4 Jesus, my shepherd, brother, friend,
   my prophet, priest and king;
   my Lord, my life, my way, my end –
   accept the praise I bring,
   (accept the praise I bring.)

5 Though weak my love and poor my care,
   though cold my warmest thought:
   yet when I see you as you are,
   I'll praise you as I ought.

6 Till then I would your love proclaim
   with every fleeting breath:
   and may the music of your name
   refresh my soul in death,
   (refresh my soul in death.)

The last line of verses 2, 4 and 6 is sung twice
when the tune RACHEL is used

130 Frances Havergal

1 I am trusting you, Lord Jesus,
   you have died for me;
   trusting you for full salvation
   great and free.

2 I am trusting you for pardon –
   at your feet I bow;
   for your grace and tender mercy,
   trusting now.

3 I am trusting you for cleansing,
   Jesus, Son of God;
   trusting you to make me holy
   by your blood.

4 I am trusting you to guide me –
   you alone shall lead;
   every day and hour supplying
   all my need.

5 I am trusting you for power –
   yours can never fail;
   words which you yourself shall give me
   must prevail.

6 I am trusting you, Lord Jesus –
   never let me fall;
   I am trusting you for ever,
   and for all.

131 © Michael Perry / Jubilate Hymns

1 I believe in God the Father
   who created heaven and earth,
   holding all things in his power,
   bringing light and life to birth.

2 I believe in God the Saviour,
   Son of Man and Lord most high,
   crucified to be redeemer,
   raised to life that death may die.

3 I believe in God the Spirit,
   wind of heaven and flame of fire,
   pledge of all that we inherit,
   sent to comfort and inspire.

4 Honour, glory, might and merit
   be to God, and God alone!
   Father, Son and Holy Spirit,
   One-in-Three and Three-in-One.

132 Brian Wren
© Oxford University Press

1 I come with joy to meet my Lord,
   forgiven, loved and free;
   in awe and wonder to recall
   his life laid down for me.

2 I come with Christians far and near
   to find, as all are fed,
   the new community of love
   in Christ's communion bread.

3 As Christ breaks bread and bids us share,
each proud division ends;
the love that made us makes us one,
and strangers now are friends.

4 And thus with joy we meet our Lord;
his presence, always near,
is in such friendship better known:
we see and praise him here.

5 Together met, together bound,
we'll go our different ways;
and as his people in the world
we'll live and speak his praise.

133 Samuel Medley

1 I know that my redeemer lives –
what comfort this assurance gives!
He lives, he lives, who once was dead,
he lives, my everlasting head.

2 He lives, triumphant from the grave,
he lives, eternally to save;
he lives, to bless me with his love,
and intercedes for me above.

3 He lives to help in time of need,
he lives, my hungry soul to feed;
he lives, and grants me daily breath,
he lives, and I shall conquer death.

4 He lives, my kind, wise, constant friend,
who still will guard me to the end;
he lives, and while he lives I'll sing,
Jesus, my prophet, priest and king!

5 He lives, my saviour, to prepare
a place in heaven, and lead me there;
he lives – all glory to his name,
Jesus, unchangeably the same.

134 From Psalm 18
© Christopher Idle / Jubilate Hymns

1 I love you, O Lord, you alone,
my refuge on whom I depend;
my maker, my saviour, my own,
my hope and my trust without end:
the Lord is my strength and my song,
defender and guide of my ways;
my master to whom I belong,
my God who shall have all my praise.

2 The dangers of death gathered round,
the waves of destruction came near;
but in my despairing I found
the Lord who released me from fear:
I called for his help in my pain,
to God my salvation I cried:
he brought me his comfort again,
I live by the strength he supplied.

3 The earth and the elements shake
with thunder and lightning and hail;
the cliffs and the mountaintops break
and mortals are feeble and pale.
His justice is full and complete,
his mercy to us has no end;
the clouds are a path for his feet,
he comes on the wings of the wind.

4 My hope is the promise he gives,
my life is secure in his hand;
I shall not be lost, for he lives!
he comes to my aid – I shall stand!
Lord God, you are powerful to save,
your Spirit will spur me to pray;
your Son has defeated the grave:
I trust and I praise you today!

135 William Fullerton

1 I cannot tell why he whom angels worship
should set his love upon our wayward world,
or why as shepherd
    he should seek the wanderers,
to bring them back into his flock and fold.
But this I know, that he was born of Mary
when Bethlehem's manger was his only home,
and that he lived at Nazareth and laboured;
and so the saviour, saviour of the world,
    has come.

2 I cannot tell how silently he suffered
as with his peace he graced this place of tears,
nor how his heart upon the cross was broken,
the crown of pain to three and thirty years.
But this I know, he heals the broken-hearted
and stays our sin and calms our lurking fear,
and lifts the burden from the heavy-laden;
for still the saviour, saviour of the world,
    is here.

3   I cannot tell how he will win the nations,
    how he will claim his earthly heritage,
    how satisfy the needs and aspirations
    of east and west, of sinner and of sage.
    But this I know, all flesh shall see his glory,
    and he shall reap the harvest he has sown,
    and some glad day
        his sun will shine in splendour
    when he the saviour, saviour of the world,
        is known.

4   I cannot tell how all the lands shall worship,
    when at his bidding every storm is stilled,
    or who can say how great the jubilation
    when all our hearts
        with love for him are filled.
    But this I know,
        the skies will sound his praises,
    and myriad, myriad human voices sing,
    and earth to heaven, and heaven to earth
        will answer,
    'At last the saviour, saviour of the world,
        is king!'

136 From 1 Corinthians 15
         © Christopher Idle / Jubilate Hymns

1   If Christ had not been raised from death
    our faith would be in vain,
    our preaching but a waste of breath,
    our sin and guilt remain.
        But now the Lord is risen indeed;
        he rules in earth and heaven:
        his Gospel meets a world of need –
        in Christ we are forgiven.

2   If Christ still lay within the tomb
    then death would be the end,
    and we should face our final doom
    with neither guide nor friend.
        But now the Saviour is raised up,
        so when a Christian dies
        we mourn, yet look to God in hope –
        in Christ the saints arise!

3   If Christ had not been truly raised
    his church would live a lie;
    his name should never more be praised,
    his words deserve to die.
        But now our great Redeemer lives;
        through him we are restored;
        his word endures, his church revives
        in Christ, our risen Lord.

137 Walter Smith
         © in this version Jubilate Hymns

1   Immortal, invisible, God only wise,
    in light inaccessible hid from our eyes;
    most holy, most glorious, the ancient of days,
    almighty, victorious,
        your great name we praise.

2   Unresting, unhasting, and silent as light,
    nor wanting, nor wasting,
        you rule us in might;
    your justice
        like mountains high soaring above,
    your clouds
        which are fountains of goodness and love.

3   To all you are giving, to life great and small,
    in all you are living, the true life of all:
    we blossom and flourish, uncertain and frail;
    we wither and perish, but you never fail.

4   We worship before you, great Father of light,
    while angels adore you, all veiling their sight;
    our praises we render, O Father, to you
    whom only the splendour of light
        hides from view.

138 © Michael Saward / Jubilate Hymns

1   In awe and wonder, Lord our God,
    we bow before your throne;
    such holiness and burning love
    are yours, and yours alone.

2   Angelic spirits, night and day,
    adore your name on high.
    Eternal Lord in majesty
    you hear their ceaseless cry:

3   'O holy, holy, holy Lord,
    great God of power and might,
    all-glorious in heaven and earth,
    you reign in realms of light.'

4   Your holiness inspires our fear,
    evokes, and heals, our shame;
    your boundless wisdom, awesome power,
    unchangeably the same.

5   Salvation comes from you alone
    which we can never win;
    your love revealed on Calvary
    is cleansing for our sin.

6   There is no grace to match your grace,
    no love to match your love,
    no gentleness of human touch
    like that of heaven above.

7 On earth we long for heaven's joy
   where, bowed before your throne,
   we know you, Father, Spirit, Son,
   as God, and God alone.

139 After John Bowring
© in this version Word & Music / Jubilate Hymns

1 In the cross of Christ I glory
   towering over wrecks of time;
   all the light of sacred story
   gathers round his head sublime.

2 When earth's sorrows overtake me,
   hopes deceive and fears annoy,
   never shall the cross forsake me –
   Christ shall bring me peace and joy.

3 When the sun of bliss is beaming
   light and life upon my way,
   from the cross his radiance streaming
   adds more lustre to the day.

4 Joy and sorrow, pain and pleasure
   by the cross are sanctified;
   peace is there beyond all measure
   through the grace of Christ who died.

140 Jamie Owens-Collins
© 1984 Fairhill Music / Word Music (UK) /
CopyCare Ltd

1 In heavenly armour we'll enter the land –
   the battle belongs to the Lord;
   no weapon that's fashioned against us will
        stand –
   the battle belongs to the Lord.
      And we sing glory, honour,
      power and strength to the Lord;
      we sing glory, honour,
      power and strength to the Lord!

2 When the power of darkness
        comes in like a flood,
   the battle belongs to the Lord;
   he's raised up a standard,
        the power of his blood –
   the battle belongs to the Lord.
      And we sing glory . . .

3 When your enemy presses in hard,
        do not fear –
   the battle belongs to the Lord;
   take courage, my friend,
        your redemption is near –
   the battle belongs to the Lord.
      And we sing glory . . .
      and we sing glory . . .
      Power and strength to the Lord,
      power and strength to the Lord!

141 Anna Waring
© in this version Jubilate Hymns

1 In heavenly love abiding,
   no change my heart shall fear;
   and safe is such confiding,
   for nothing changes here:
   the storm may roar around me,
   my heart may low be laid;
   my Father's arms surround me,
   how can I be afraid?
      (In heavenly love abiding,
      no change my heart shall fear;
      and safe is such confiding,
      for nothing changes here.)

2 Wherever he may guide me
   no want shall turn me back;
   my shepherd is beside me
   and nothing can I lack:
   his wisdom is for ever,
   his sight is never dim;
   his love deserts me never
   and I will walk with him.
      (In heavenly love . . .)

3 Green pastures are before me,
   which yet I have not seen;
   bright skies will shine with glory
   where threatening clouds have been:
   my hope I cannot measure,
   my path to life is free;
   my saviour has my treasure,
   and he will walk with me.
      (In heavenly love . . .)

The chorus is not sung when the tune PENLAN is used

142 © Christopher Idle / Jubilate Hymns

1 In silent pain the eternal Son
        hangs derelict and still;
   in darkened day his work is done,
        fulfilled, his Father's will.
      Uplifted for the world to see
      he hangs in strangest victory,
      for in his body on the tree
      he carries all our ill.

2 He died that we might die to sin
        and live for righteousness;
   the earth is stained, to make us clean
        and bring us into peace.
      For peace he came, and met its cost;
      he gave himself to save the lost;
      he loved us to the uttermost
      and paid for our release.

3 For strife he came, to bring a sword,
   the truth to end all lies;
to rule in us, our patient Lord,
   until all evil dies:
      for in his hand he holds the stars,
      his voice shall speak to end our wars,
      and those who love him see his scars
      and look into his eyes.

143 Edmund Sears
© in this version Jubilate Hymns

1 It came upon the midnight clear,
   that glorious song of old,
from angels bending near the earth
to touch their harps of gold:
'Upon the earth, goodwill and peace
from heaven's all-gracious king!'
The world in solemn stillness lay
to hear the angels sing.

2 With sorrow brought by sin and strife
the world has suffered long
and, since the angels sang, have passed
two thousand years of wrong:
the nations, still at war, hear not
the love-song which they bring:
O hush the noise and cease the strife,
to hear the angels sing!

3 All those whose journey now is hard,
whose hope is burning low,
who tread the rocky path of life
with painful steps and slow:
O listen to the news of love
which makes the heavens ring;
O rest beside the weary road
and hear the angels sing!

4 And still the days are hastening on –
by prophets seen of old –
towards the fulness of the time
when comes the age foretold;
then earth and heaven renewed shall see
the prince of peace, their king –
and all the world repeat the song
which now the angels sing.

144 William How
© in this version Jubilate Hymns

1 It is a thing most wonderful –
almost too wonderful to be –
that God's own Son should come from heaven
and die to save a child like me.

2 And yet I know that it is true:
he came to this poor world below,
and wept and toiled, and mourned and died,
only because he loved us so.

3 I cannot tell how he could love
a child so weak and full of sin;
his love must be most wonderful
if he could die my love to win.

4 I sometimes think about the cross,
and shut my eyes, and try to see
the cruel nails, and crown of thorns,
and Jesus crucified for me.

5 But, even could I see him die,
I could but see a little part
of that great love which, like a fire,
is always burning in his heart.

6 How wonderful it is to see
my love for him so faint and poor,
but yet more wonderful to know
his love for me so free and sure.

7 And yet I want to love you, Lord:
O teach me how to grow in grace,
that I may love you more and more
until I see you face to face!

145 © Michael Saward / Jubilate Hymns

1 Jesus Christ gives life and gladness
to a world of death and grief;
love, to conquer human madness,
and, to broken hearts, relief;
hope for doubt and joy for sadness,
faith to silence unbelief.

2 Jesus in his incarnation
took our flesh, unique, alone;
on the cross won our salvation
nailed there to a wooden throne;
rising, laid the true foundation
of his church, a living stone.

3 Jesus works through us, expressing
to the nations in their need
his great love; that all possessing
faith and hope, from bondage freed,
round the globe may join, confessing.
'Jesus Christ is life indeed.'

146 Unknown

1 Jesus Christ is risen today,
   Alleluia,
our triumphant holy day;
   alleluia,
who did once upon the cross
   alleluia,
suffer to redeem our loss.
   alleluia!

2 Hymns of joy then let us sing
   Alleluia,
praising Christ our heavenly king;
   alleluia,
who endured the cross and grave
   alleluia,
sinners to redeem and save!
   alleluia!

3 But the pains which he endured
   Alleluia,
our salvation have procured;
   alleluia,
now above the sky he's king
   alleluia,
where the angels ever sing.
   alleluia!

147
After German authors
© Michael Perry / Jubilee Hymns

1 Jesus Christ the Lord is born,
all the bells are ringing!
angels greet the holy One
   and shepherds hear them singing,
   and shepherds hear them singing.

2 'Go to Bethlehem today,
find your king and saviour:
glory be to God on high,
   to earth his peace and favour,
   to earth his peace and favour!'

3 Held within a cattle stall,
loved by love maternal,
see the master of us all,
   our Lord of lords eternal,
   our Lord of lords eternal.

4 Soon shall come the wise men three,
rousing Herod's anger;
mother's hearts shall broken be
   and Mary's son in danger,
   and Mary's son in danger.

5 Death from life and life from death,
our salvation's story:
let all living things give breath
   to Christmas songs of glory,
   to Christmas songs of glory!

148
From John 2
© Christopher Idle / Jubilee Hymns

1 Jesus, come! for we invite you,
guest and master, friend and Lord;
now, as once at Cana's wedding,
speak, and let us hear your word:
lead us through our need or doubting,
hope be born and joy restored.

2 Jesus, come! transform our pleasures,
guide us into paths unknown;
bring your gifts, command your servants,
let us trust in you alone:
though your hand may work in secret,
all shall see what you have done.

3 Jesus, come in new creation,
heaven brought near in power divine;
give your unexpected glory
changing water into wine:
rouse the faith of your disciples –
come, our first and greatest Sign!

4 Jesus, come! surprise our dullness,
make us willing to receive
more than we can yet imagine,
all the best you have to give:
let us find your hidden riches,
taste your love, believe, and live!

149
After John Cennick
Charles Wesley and Martin Madan
© in this version Jubilee Hymns

1 Jesus comes with clouds descending:
see the Lamb for sinners slain!
Thousand thousand saints attending
join to sing the glad refrain –
   Alleluia, alleluia, alleluia!
God appears on earth to reign.

2 Every eye shall then behold him
robed in awesome majesty;
those who jeered at him and sold him,
pierced and nailed him to the tree,
   shamed and grieving,
   shamed and grieving,
   shamed and grieving
shall their true Messiah see.

3 All the wounds of cross and passion
still his glorious body bears;
cause of endless exultation
to his ransomed worshippers.
   With what gladness,
   with what gladness,
   with what gladness
we shall see the Saviour's scars!

4 Yes, Amen! Let all adore you
high on your eternal throne;
crowns and empires fall before you –
claim the kingdom for your own.
   Come, Lord Jesus,
   come, Lord Jesus,
   come, Lord Jesus
everlasting God, come down!

150
From the Latin
verses 1 and 2 John Neale
verses 3 and 4 Percy Dearmer

1 Jesus, good above all other,
gentle child of gentle mother;
in a stable born our brother,
whom the angel hosts adore:

2 Jesus, cradled in a manger,
keep us free from sin and danger;
and to all, both friend and stranger,
give your blessing evermore.

3 Jesus, for your people dying,
risen master, death defying;
Lord of heaven, your grace supplying,
come to us – be present here!

4 Lord, in all our doings guide us:
pride and hate shall not divide us;
we'll go on with you beside us,
and with joy we'll persevere.

151
Wendy Churchill
© 1981 Springtide / Word Music (UK) / CopyCare Ltd

1 Jesus is king, and we will extol him,
give him the glory, and honour his name;
he reigns on high, enthroned in the heavens –
Word of the Father, exalted for us.

2 We have a hope that is steadfast and certain,
gone through the curtain
     and touching the throne;
we have a Priest who is there interceding,
pouring his grace on our lives day by day.

3 We come to him our Priest and Apostle,
clothed in his glory and bearing his name,
laying our lives with gladness before him –
filled with his Spirit we worship the King:

4 'O Holy One, our hearts do adore you;
thrilled with your goodness
     we give you our praise!'
Angels in light with worship surround him,
Jesus, our Saviour, for ever the same.

152
Tom Colvin
© 1969, 1980 Hope Publishing Company

Jesus, Jesus, fill us with your love;
show us how to serve
     the neighbours we have from you.

1 Kneels at the feet of his friends,
silently washes their feet –
Master who acts as a slave to them:
     Jesus, Jesus . . .

2 Neighbours are rich folk and poor;
neighbours are black, brown and white;
neighbours are nearby and far away:
     Jesus, Jesus . . .

3 These are the ones we should serve,
these are the ones we should love;
all these are neighbours to us and you:
     Jesus, Jesus . . .

4 Loving puts us on our knees,
serving as though we were slaves –
this is the way we should live with you:
     Jesus, Jesus . . .

153
After Christian Gellert, Frances Cox
© in this version Jubilate Hymns

1 Jesus lives! Your terrors now
can, O death, no more appal us:
Jesus lives! – by this we know
you, O grave, cannot enthral us:
     Alleluia!

2 Jesus lives! – henceforth is death
but the gate of life immortal;
this shall calm our trembling breath
when we pass its gloomy portal:
     Alleluia!

3 Jesus lives! – for us he died:
then, alone to Jesus living,
pure in heart may we abide,
glory to our saviour giving:
     Alleluia!

4 Jesus lives! – this bond of love
neither life nor death shall sever,
powers in hell or heaven above
tear us from his keeping never:
     Alleluia!

5 Jesus lives! – to him the throne
over all the world is given;
may we go where he is gone,
rest and reign with him in heaven:
     Alleluia!

154
Charles Wesley

1 Jesus, lover of my soul,
let me to your presence fly,
while the gathering waters roll,
while the tempest still is high.
Hide me, O my Saviour, hide,
till the storm of life is past;
safe into the haven, guide
and receive my soul at last.

2 Other refuge have I none,
  all my hope in you I see:
  leave, O leave me, not alone;
  still support and comfort me.
  All my trust on you is stayed,
  all my help from you I bring:
  cover my defenceless head
  with the shadow of your wing.

3 You, O Christ, are all I want,
  more than all in you I find:
  raise the fallen, cheer the faint,
  heal the sick and lead the blind.
  Just and holy is your name,
  I am all unworthiness;
  false and full of sin I am,
  you are full of truth and grace,

4 Plenteous grace with you is found,
  grace to wash away my sin:
  let the healing streams abound;
  make and keep me clean within.
  Living Fountain, now impart
  all your life and purity;
  spring for ever in my heart,
  rise to all eternity!

155 © Michael Perry / Jubilate Hymns

1 Jesus, saviour, holy child, sleep tonight,
  slumber deep till morning light.
    Lullaby, our joy, our treasure,
    all our hope and all our pleasure:
  at the cradle where you lie
  we will worship – lullaby!

2 From your Father's home you come
      to this earth,
  by your lowly manger birth!
    Child of God, our nature sharing;
    Son of Man, our sorrows bearing;
  rich, yet here among the poor:
  Christ the Lord, whom we adore!

3 Now to heaven's glory song we reply
  with a Christmas lullaby.
    Hush, the eternal Lord is sleeping
    close in Mary's tender keeping:
  babe on whom the angels smiled –
  Jesus, saviour, holy child.

156 Isaac Watts
© in this version Jubilate Hymns

1 Jesus shall reign where'er the sun
  does its successive journeys run;
  his kingdom stretch from shore to shore
  till moons shall rise and set no more.

2 People and realms of every tongue
  declare his love in sweetest song,
  and children's voices shall proclaim
  their early blessings on his name.

3 Blessings abound where Jesus reigns –
  the prisoner leaps to lose his chains,
  the weary find eternal rest,
  the hungry and the poor are blessed.

4 To him shall endless prayer be made,
  and princes throng to crown his head;
  his name like incense shall arise
  with every morning sacrifice.

5 Let all creation rise and bring
  the highest honours to our king;
  angels descend with songs again
  and earth repeat the loud 'Amen!'

157 William Pennefather

1 Jesus, stand among us
  in your risen power;
  let this time of worship
  be a hallowed hour.

2 Breathe the Holy Spirit
  into every heart;
  bid the fears and sorrows
  from each soul depart.

3 This with quickened footsteps
  we'll pursue our way,
  watching for the dawning
  of eternal day.

158 From the Latin
Ray Palmer

1 Jesus, the joy of loving hearts,
  true source of life, our lives sustain:
  from the best bliss that earth imparts
  we turn unfilled to you again.

2 Your truth unchanged has ever stood,
  you rescue those who on you call:
  to those yet seeking, you are good –
  to those who find you, all-in-all.

3 We taste of you, the living bread,
  and long to feast upon you still;
  we drink from you, the fountain-head,
  our thirsty souls from you we fill.

4 Our restless spirits long for you,
  whichever way our lot is cast,
  glad when your gracious smile we view,
  blessed when our faith can hold you fast.

5 Jesus, for ever with us stay,
make all our moments calm and bright;
chase the dark night of sin away,
spread through the world your holy light.

159 Charles Wesley

1 Jesus! the name high over all
in hell or earth or sky;
angels again before it fall
and devils fear and fly,
and devils fear and fly.

2 Jesus! the name to sinners dear,
the name to sinners given;
it scatters all their guilty fear,
it turns their hell to heaven,
it turns their hell to heaven!

3 Jesus the prisoner's fetters breaks
and bruises Satan's head;
power into strengthless souls he speaks
and life into the dead,
and life into the dead.

4 O that the world might taste and see
the riches of his grace!
The arms of love that welcome me
would everyone embrace,
would everyone embrace.

5 His righteousness alone I show,
his saving grace proclaim;
this is my work on earth below,
to cry 'Behold the Lamb!'
to cry 'Behold the Lamb!'

6 Happy if with my final breath
I may but gasp his name,
preach him to all, and cry in death,
'Behold, behold the Lamb!'
'Behold, behold the Lamb!'

160 Margaret Clarkson
© 1983 Hope Publishing Company

1 Jesus the saviour comes!
Greet him with joyful song,
prince of the heavenly throne,
promised to earth so long:
he comes to fight our mortal foe
and carry all our sin and woe.

2 Jesus the saviour comes!
Lord over life and death;
sin and destruction die,
felled by his holy breath:
triumphant from the cross and grave
he comes to heal and bless and save.

3 Jesus the saviour comes!
sovereign and Lord of all;
kingdoms, dominions, powers –
all at his feet must fall:
he comes to banish death and sin
and bring his great salvation in.

4 Lord of the Christmas crib,
Lord of the cross of shame,
humbly we worship you,
proudly we take your name:
be all our joy till advent drums
and trumpets cry, 'The saviour comes!'

5 Then with your ransomed hosts,
faultless before your face,
sons of the living God,
born of redeeming grace,
your love we'll sing, your power we'll praise:
your name adore through endless days!

161 Isaac Watts

1 Joy to the world! The Lord has come:
let earth receive her king,
let every heart prepare him room
and heaven and nature sing,
and heaven and nature sing,
and heaven, and heaven and nature sing!

2 Joy to the earth! The saviour reigns:
your sweetest songs employ
while fields and streams and hills and plains
repeat the sounding joy,
repeat the sounding joy,
repeat, repeat the sounding joy.

3 He rules the world with truth and grace,
and makes the nations prove
the glories of his righteousness,
the wonders of his love,
the wonders of his love,
the wonders, wonders of his love.

162 Henry Holland
© in this version Jubilate Hymns

1 Judge eternal, throned in splendour,
Lord of lords and King of kings,
with your living fire of judgement
purge this realm of bitter things;
comfort all its wide dominion
with the healing of your wings.

2 Weary people still are longing
for the hour that brings release,
and the city's crowded clamour
cries aloud for sin to cease;
and the countryside and woodlands
plead in silence for their peace.

3 Crown, O Lord, your own endeavour,
cleave our darkness with your sword,
cheer the faint and feed the hungry
with the richness of your word;
cleanse the body of this nation
through the glory of the Lord.

163 From Psalm 42, John Bell and Graham Maule
© 1989 Wild Goose Publications / Iona Community

1 Just as a lost and thirsty deer
longs for the cool and running stream,
I thirst for you, the living God,
anxious to know that you are near.

2 Both day and night I cry aloud;
tears have become my only food
while all around cruel voices ask,
'Where is your God, where is your God?'

3 Broken and hurt I call to mind
how in the past I served the Lord,
worshipped and walked with happy crowds,
singing and shouting praise to God.

4 Why am I now so lost and low;
why am I troubled and confused?
Given no answer, still I hope
and trust my Saviour and my God.

164 Charlotte Elliott
© in this version Jubilee Hymns

1 Just as I am, without one plea
but that you died to set me free,
and at your bidding 'Come to me!'
O Lamb of God, I come, I come.

2 Just as I am, without delay
your call of mercy I obey –
your blood can wash my sins away:
O Lamb of God, I come, I come.

3 Just as I am, though tossed about
with many a conflict, many a doubt,
fightings within and fears without,
O Lamb of God, I come, I come.

4 Just as I am, poor, wretched, blind!
Sight, riches, healing of the mind –
all that I need, in you to find,
O Lamb of God, I come, I come.

5 Just as I am! You will receive,
will welcome, pardon, cleanse, relieve:
because your promise I believe,
O Lamb of God, I come, I come.

6 Just am I am! Your love unknown
has broken every barrier down:
now to be yours, yes, yours alone,
O Lamb of God, I come, I come.

7 Just as I am! Of that free love
the breadth, length, depth and height
to prove,
here for a time and then above,
O Lamb of God, I come, I come.

165 George Herbert
© in this version Word & Music / Jubilate Hymns

1 King of glory, king of peace
I will love you;
since your mercies never cease,
faith shall prove you!
You have granted my request,
you have heard me;
though my sinful soul transgressed,
you have spared me.

2 Praises with my utmost art
I will bring you;
songs of triumph from my heart
I will sing you.
Though my sins against me cried,
this shall cheer me:
God in Christ has justified
and will clear me.

3 Seven whole days – not one in seven –
I will praise you;
worship lifts the heart to heaven,
love obeys you!
Once you died, when no-one sought
to console you;
now eternity's too short
to extol you!

166 © Michael Saward / Jubilate Hymns

1 King of the universe, Lord of the ages,
maker of all things, sustainer of life;
source of authority, wise and just creator,
hope of the nations: we praise and adore,
we praise and adore.

2 Powerful in majesty, throned in the heavens –
sun, moon and stars by your word are upheld;
time and eternity bow within your presence,
Lord of the nations: we praise and adore,
we praise and adore.

3 Wisdom unsearchable, fathomless knowledge
 past understanding by our clever brain;
 ground of reality, basis of all order,
 guide to the nations: we praise and adore,
  we praise and adore.

4 Justice and righteousness, holy, unswerving –
 all that is tainted shall burn in your flame;
 sword-bearing deity, punisher of evil,
 judge of the nations: we praise and adore,
  we praise and adore.

5 Ruler and potentate, sage and lawgiver,
 humbled before you, unworthy we bow:
 in our extremity, show us your forgiveness,
 merciful Father: we praise and adore,
  we praise and adore.

167 James Edmeston
© in this version Jubilate Hymns

1 Lead us, heavenly Father, lead us
  through this world's tempestuous sea;
 guard us, guide us, keep us, feed us,
  now and to eternity:
 here possessing every blessing
  if our God our Father be.

2 Saviour, by your grace restore us –
  all our weaknesses are plain:
 you have lived on earth before us,
  you have felt our grief and pain.
 Tempted, taunted, yet undaunted,
  from the depths you rose again.

3 Spirit of our God, descending,
  fill our hearts with holy peace –
 love with every passion blending,
  pleasure that can never cease:
 thus provided, pardoned, guided,
  ever shall our joys increase.

168 Graham Kendrick
© 1983 Thankyou Music

1 Led like a lamb to the slaughter
 in silence and shame,
 there on your back
 you carried a world
 of violence and pain,
  bleeding, dying,
  bleeding, dying.
  You're alive – you're alive,
  you have risen –
   Alleluia . . .
  and the power
  and the glory is given –
   Alleluia . . .
  Jesus to you.

2 At break of dawn – poor Mary,
 still weeping, she came:
 when through her grief
 she heard your voice
 now speaking her name,
  A 'Mary!' B 'Master!'
  A 'Mary!' B 'Master!'
  You're alive . . .

3 At the right hand of the Father,
 now seated on high,
 you have begun your eternal reign
 of justice and joy:
  Glory, glory,
  glory, glory!
  You're alive . . .

The congregation may divide at A and B

169 From Psalm 67, Christopher Rolinson
© 1988 Thankyou Music

ALL Let the people praise you, O God,
A   let all the people praise you,
B   let all the people praise you.
ALL Let the people praise you, O God,
A   let all the people praise you,
B   let all the people praise you,
ALL let all the people praise you.

1 May your ways be known on earth,
 and your power to save us:
 then the peoples of the world
 shall fear you, shall fear you.
  ALL Let the people . . .

2 We'll be glad and sing for joy,
 for you rule with justice;
 then the ends of all the earth
 shall fear you, shall fear you.
  ALL Let the people . . .

3 For you are a gracious God,
 we delight to praise you:
 then our land shall see
 the fruits of blessing, your blessing.
  ALL Let the people . . .

The congregation may divide at A and B

170 Phillip Doddridge

1 Let trumpets sound! The Saviour comes,
 the Saviour promised long:
 let every heart prepare a throne
 and every voice a song!

2   He comes the prisoners to release
in Satan's bondage held;
the gates of brass before him burst,
the iron fetters yield.

3   He comes the broken heart to bind,
the wounded soul to cure;
and with the treasures of his grace
to enrich the humble poor.

4   Our glad hosannas, Prince of peace,
your welcome shall proclaim;
and heaven's eternal arches ring
with your belovèd name.

171   John Newton

1   Let us love and sing and wonder;
let us praise the saviour's name!
he has hushed the law's loud thunder;
he has quenched Mount Sinai's flame:
he has freed us by his blood;
he has brought us nearer God.

2   Let us love the Lord who bought us,
dying for our rebel race;
called us by his word and taught us
by the Spirit of his grace:
he has freed us by his blood;
he presents our souls to God.

3   Let us sing, though fierce temptation
threatens hard to drag us down;
for the Lord, our strong salvation,
holds in view the conqueror's crown:
he who freed us by his blood,
soon will bring us home to God.

4   Let us wonder at the glory
God will lavish on his own;
saved by grace, we tell the story
of the cross, the grave, the crown:
'You have freed us by your blood,
you are worthy, Lamb of God!'

172   From Psalm 95
© Richard Bewes / Jubilate Hymns

1   Let us sing to the God of salvation,
let us sing to the Lord our rock;
let us come to his house with thanksgiving,
let us come before the Lord and sing!
Praise our maker,
praise our saviour,
praise the Lord
our everlasting king:
every throne
must bow before him –
God is Lord of everything!

2   In his hand are the earth's deepest places,
and the strength of the hills is his;
all the sea is the Lord's, for he made it –
by his hand the solid rock was formed.
Praise our maker . . .

3   Let us worship the Lord our maker,
let us kneel to the Lord our God;
for we all are the sheep of his pasture –
he will guide us by his powerful hand.
Praise our maker . . .

4   Let today be the time when you hear him!
May our hearts not be hard or cold,
lest we stray from the Lord in rebellion
as his people did in time of old.
Praise our maker . . .

173   Carl P Daw Jr.
© 1982 Hope Publishing Company

1   Like the murmur of the dove's song,
like the challenge of her flight,
like the vigour of the wind's rush,
like the new flame's eager might:
come, Holy Spirit, come.

2   To the members of Christ's Body,
to the branches of the Vine,
to the Church in faith assembled,
to her midst as gift and sign:
come, Holy Spirit, come.

3   With the healing of division,
with the ceaseless voice of prayer,
with the power to love and witness,
with the peace beyond compare:
come, Holy Spirit, come.

174   From Psalm 5, Brian Foley
© 1971 Faber Music Ltd

1   Lord, as I wake I turn to you,
yourself the first thought of my day;
my king, my God, whose help is sure,
yourself the help for which I pray.

2   There is no blessing, Lord, from you
for those who make their will their way,
no praise for those who will not praise,
no peace for those who will not pray.

3   Your loving gifts of grace to me,
those favours I could never earn,
call for my thanks in praise and prayer,
call me to love you in return.

4   Lord, make my life a life of love,
keep me from sin in all I do;
Lord, make your law my only law,
your will my will, for love of you.

175
From the Irish
Mary Byrne and Eleanor Hull
© in this version Jubilate Hymns

1 Lord, be my vision, supreme in my heart;
   bid every rival give way and depart:
   you my best thought in the day or the night,
   waking or sleeping, your presence my light.

2 Lord, be my wisdom and be my true word;
   I ever with you and you with me, Lord:
   you my great father and I your true child,
   once far away, but by love reconciled.

3 Lord, be my breastplate,
        my sword for the fight;
   be my strong armour, for you are my might.
   You are my shelter and you my high tower –
   raise me to heaven, O Power of my power.

4 I need no riches, nor earth's empty praise –
   you my inheritance through all my days;
   all of your treasure to me you impart,
   high King of heaven, the first in my heart.

5 High King of heaven, when battle is done,
   grant heaven's joy to me, bright heaven's sun;
   Christ of my own heart, whatever befall,
   still be my vision, O Ruler of all.

176
© Timothy Dudley-Smith

1 Lord, for the years
        your love has kept and guided,
   urged and inspired us, cheered us on our way,
   sought us and saved us,
        pardoned and provided,
   Lord of the years, we bring our thanks today.

2 Lord, for that word,
        the word of life which fires us,
   speaks to our hearts and sets our souls ablaze;
   teaches and trains, rebukes us and inspires us;
   Lord of the word,
        receive your people's praise.

3 Lord, for our land, in this our generation,
   spirits oppressed
        by pleasure, wealth and care;
   for young and old,
        for commonwealth and nation,
   Lord of our land,
        be pleased to hear our prayer.

4 Lord, for our world;
        when we disown and doubt him,
   loveless in strength, and comfortless in pain;
   hungry and helpless, lost indeed without him;
   Lord of the world,
        we pray that Christ may reign.

5 Lord, for ourselves;
        in living power remake us –
   self on the cross and Christ upon the throne,
   past put behind us, for the future take us,
   Lord of our lives, to live for Christ alone.

177
William Matson
© in this version Jubilate Hymns

1 Lord, I was blind; I could not see
   in your marred visage any grace:
   but now the beauty of your face
   in radiant vision dawns on me.

2 Lord, I was deaf; I could not hear
   the thrilling music of your voice:
   but now I hear you and rejoice,
   and all your spoken words are dear.

3 Lord, I was dumb; I could not speak
   the grace and glory of your name:
   but now as touched with living flame
   my lips will speak for Jesus' sake.

4 Lord, I was dead; I could not move
   my lifeless soul from sin's dark grave:
   but now the power of life you gave
   has raised me up to know your love.

5 Lord, you have made the blind to see,
   the deaf to hear, the dumb to speak,
   the dead to live – and now I break
   the chains of my captivity!

178
Patrick Appleford
© 1960 Josef Weinberger Ltd

1 Lord Jesus Christ, you have come to us,
   you are one with us, Mary's son;
   cleansing our souls from all their sin,
   pouring your love and goodness in:
   Jesus, our love for you we sing –
        living Lord!

2 Lord Jesus Christ, you have come to us,
   born as one of us, Mary's son;
   led out to die on Calvary,
   risen from death to set us free:
   living Lord Jesus, help us see
        you are Lord!

AT COMMUNION THIS MAY BE SUNG

3 Lord Jesus Christ, now and every day
   teach us how to pray, Son of God;
   you have commanded us to do
   this in remembrance, Lord, of you:
   into our lives your power breaks through
        living Lord!

4 Lord Jesus Christ, I would come to you,
  live my life for you, Son of God;
  all your commands I know are true,
  your many gifts will make me new:
  into my life your power breaks through –
      living Lord!

179 © Michael Perry / Jubilee Hymns

1 Like a mighty river flowing,
  like a flower in beauty growing,
  far beyond all human knowing
      is the perfect peace of God.

2 Like the hills serene and even,
  like the coursing clouds of heaven,
  like the heart that's been forgiven
      is the perfect peace of God.

3 Like the summer breezes playing,
  like the tall trees softly swaying,
  like the lips of silent praying
      is the perfect peace of God.

4 Like the morning sun ascended,
  like the scents of evening blended,
  like a friendship never ended
      is the perfect peace of God.

5 Like the azure ocean swelling,
  like the jewel all-excelling,
  far beyond our human telling
      is the perfect peace of God.

180 © Timothy Dudley-Smith

1 Lord of the church, we pray for our renewing:
  Christ over all, our undivided aim.
  Fire of the Spirit, burn for our enduing,
  wind of the Spirit, fan the living flame!
  We turn to Christ amid our fear and failing,
  that will that lacks the courage to be free,
  the weary labours, all but unavailing,
  to bring us nearer what a church should be.

2 Lord of the church,
      we seek a Father's blessing,
  a true repentance and a faith restored,
  a swift obedience and a new possessing,
  filled with the Holy Spirit of the Lord!
  We turn to Christ
      from all our restless striving,
  unnumbered voices with a single prayer –
  the living water for our souls' reviving,
  in Christ to live, and love and serve and care.

3 Lord of the church, we long for our uniting,
  true to one calling, by one vision stirred;
  one cross proclaiming and one creed reciting,
  one in the truth of Jesus and his word!
  So lead us on; till toil and trouble ended,
  one church triumphant
      one new song shall sing,
  to praise his glory, risen and ascended,
  Christ over all, the everlasting King!

181 © Michael Saward / Jubilee Hymns

1 Lord of the cross of shame,
  set my cold heart aflame
  with love to you, my saviour and my master;
      who on that lonely day
      bore all my sins away,
  and saved me from the judgement
      and disaster.

2 Lord of the empty tomb,
  born of a virgin's womb,
  triumphant over death, its power defeated;
      how gladly now I sing
      your praise, my risen king,
  and worship you,
      in heaven's splendour seated.

3 Lord of my life today,
  teach me to live and pray
  as one who knows the joy of sins forgiven;
      so may I ever be,
      now and eternally,
  one with my fellow-citizens in heaven.

182 Graham Kendrick
© 1987 Make Way Music

1 Lord, the light of your love is shining,
  in the midst of the darkness, shining:
  Jesus, light of the world, shine upon us;
  set us free by the truth you now bring us –
  shine on me, shine on me.
      Shine, Jesus, shine,
      fill this land with the Father's glory;
      blaze, Spirit, blaze,
      set our hearts on fire.
      Flow, river, flow,
      flood the nations with grace and mercy;
      send forth your word, Lord,
      and let there be light!

2 Lord, I come to your awesome presence,
from the shadows into your radiance;
by your Blood I may enter your brightness:
search me, try me, consume all my darkness –
shine on me, shine on me.
Shine, Jesus, shine,
fill this land with the Father's glory;
blaze, Spirit, blaze,
set our hearts on fire.
Flow, river, flow,
flood the nations with grace and mercy;
send forth your word, Lord,
and let there be light!

3 As we gaze on your kingly brightness
so our faces display your likeness,
ever changing from glory to glory:
mirrored here, may our lives tell your story –
shine on me, shine on me.
Shine, Jesus, shine . . .

183 From Acts 17
© Christopher Idle / Jubilate Hymns

1 Lord, you need no house,
no manger now, nor tomb;
yet come, I pray, to make
my heart your home,
to make my heart your home,
to make my heart your home,

2 Lord, you need no gift,
for all things come from you;
receive what you have given –
my heart renew,
my heart renew,
my heart renew.

3 Lord, you need no skill
to make your likeness known;
create your image here –
my heart your throne,
my heart your throne,
my heart your throne.

184 © Christopher Idle / Jubilate Hymns

1 Lord, you sometimes speak in wonders,
unmistakable and clear;
mighty signs to prove your presence,
overcoming doubt and fear:
O Lord, you sometimes speak in wonders.

2 Lord, you sometimes speak in whispers,
still and small and scarcely heard;
only those who want to listen
catch the all-important word:
O Lord, you sometimes speak in whispers.

3 Lord, you sometimes speak in silence,
through our loud and noisy day;
we can know and trust you better
when we quietly wait and pray:
O Lord, you sometimes speak in silence.

4 Lord, you often speak in Scripture –
words that summon from the page,
shown and taught us by your Spirit
with fresh light for every age:
O Lord, you often speak in Scripture.

5 Lord, you always speak in Jesus,
always new yet still the same:
teach us now more of our Saviour;
make our lives display his name:
O Lord, you always speak in Jesus.

The original version of this hymn text comprises the
first four lines of each verse. The fifth line was added
by the composer to fit this particular musical setting.

185 Frank Houghton
© Overseas Missionary Fellowship
and in this version Jubilate Hymns

1 Lord, you were rich beyond all splendour,
yet, for love's sake, became so poor;
leaving your throne in glad surrender,
sapphire-paved courts for stable floor:
Lord, you were rich beyond all splendour,
yet, for love's sake, became so poor.

2 You are our God beyond all praising,
yet, for love's sake, became a man;
stooping so low, but sinners raising
heavenwards, by your eternal plan:
you are our God, beyond all praising,
yet, for love's sake, became a man.

3 Lord, you are love beyond all telling,
Saviour and King, we worship you;
Emmanuel, within us dwelling,
make us and keep us pure and true:
Lord, you are love beyond all telling,
Saviour and King, we worship you.

186 Hugh Sherlock and Michael Saward
© Methodist Publishing House

1 Lord, your church on earth is seeking
power and wisdom from above:
teach us all the art of speaking
with the accents of your love.
We will heed your great commission
sending us to every place –
'Go, baptize, fulfil my mission;
serve with love and share my grace!'

2 You release us from our bondage,
lift the burdens caused by sin;
give new hope, new strength and courage,
grant release from fears within.
Light for darkness, joy for sorrow,
love for hatred, peace for strife –
these and countless blessings follow
as the Spirit gives new life.

3 In the streets of every city
where the bruised and lonely live,
we will show the saviour's pity
and his longing to forgive.
In all lands and with all races
we will serve, and seek to bring
all the world to render praises
Christ, to you, redeemer king.

187
Henry Baker
© in this version Jubilate Hymns

1 Lord, your word shall guide us
and with truth provide us:
teach us to receive it
and with joy believe it.

2 When our foes are near us,
then your word shall cheer us –
word of consolation,
message of salvation.

3 When the storms distress us
and dark clouds oppress us,
then your word protects us
and its light directs us.

4 Who can tell the pleasure,
who recount the treasure
by your word imparted
to the simple-hearted?

5 Word of mercy, giving
courage to the living;
word of life, supplying
comfort to the dying:

6 O that we discerning
its most holy learning,
Lord, may love and fear you –
evermore be near you!

188
Charles Wesley

1 Love divine, all loves excelling,
joy of heaven, to earth come down:
fix in us your humble dwelling,
all your faithful mercies crown.
Jesus, you are all compassion,
boundless love that makes us whole:
visit us with your salvation,
enter every trembling soul.

2 Come, almighty to deliver,
let us all your grace receive;
suddenly return, and never,
never more your temples leave.
You we would be always blessing,
serve you as your hosts above,
pray, and praise you without ceasing,
glory in your perfect love.

3 Finish then your new creation:
pure and sinless let us be;
let us see your great salvation,
perfect in eternity:
Changed from glory into glory
till in heaven we take our place,
there to cast our crowns before you,
lost in wonder, love and praise!

189
Luke Connaughton
© McCrimmon Publishing Co

1 Love is his word, love is his way,
feasting with all, fasting alone,
living and dying, rising again,
love, only love, is his way:
    Richer than gold is the love of my Lord,
    better than splendour and wealth.

2 Love is his way, love is his mark,
sharing his last Passover feast,
Christ at his table, host to the twelve,
love, only love, is his mark:
    Richer than gold . . .

3 Love is his mark, love is his sign,
bread for our strength, wine for our joy,
'This is my body, this is my blood' –
love, only love, is his sign:
    Richer than gold . . .

4 Love is his sign, love is his news,
'Do this,' he said, 'lest you forget.'
All his deep sorrow, all his dear blood –
love, only love, is his news:
    Richer than gold . . .

5 Love is his news, love is his name,
we are his own, chosen and called,
family, children, cousins and kin,
love, only love, is his name:
    Richer than gold . . .

6 Love is his name, love is his law,
hear his command, all who are his:
'Love one another, I have loved you' –
love, only love, is his law.
    Richer than gold . . .

7 Love is his law, love is his word:
   love of the Lord, Father and Word,
   love of the Spirit, God ever one,
   love, only love, is his word:
       Richer than gold is the love of my Lord,
       better than splendour and wealth.

*Verses 2, 3 and 4 may be omitted when
there is no communion*

190 George Robinson

1 Loved with everlasting love,
   led by grace that love to know;
   Spirit, breathing from above,
   you have taught me it is so:
   O what full and perfect peace,
   joy and wonder all divine!
   In a love which cannot cease,
       I am his and he is mine.

2 Heaven above is softer blue,
   earth around is richer green;
   something lives in every hue,
   Christless eyes have never seen:
   songs of birds in sweetness grow,
   flowers with deeper beauties shine,
   since I know, as now I know,
       I am his and he is mine.

3 His for ever, his alone!
   Who the Lord from me shall part?
   With what joy and peace unknown
   Christ can fill the loving heart!
   Heaven and earth may pass away,
   sun and stars in gloom decline,
   but of Christ I still shall say:
       I am his and he is mine.

191 Robert Lowry

1 Low in the grave he lay,
   Jesus my saviour,
   waiting the coming day,
   Jesus my Lord!
       Up from the grave he arose
       with a mighty triumph he arose;
       he arose, a victor from the dark domain,
       and he lives for ever
           with his saints to reign –
       he arose, he arose, Alleluia – Christ arose!

2 Vainly they guard his bed,
   Jesus my saviour;
   vainly they seal the dead,
   Jesus my Lord!
       Up from the grave he arose . . .

3 Death cannot keep his prey,
   Jesus my saviour;
   he tore the bars away,
   Jesus my Lord!
       Up from the grave he arose . . .

192
From the traditional prayer
Sebastian Temple, dedicated to Mrs Frances Tracy
© 1967 Franciscan Communications

1 Make me a channel of your peace:
   where there is hatred let me bring your love,
   where there is injury, your pardon, Lord,
   and where there's doubt, true faith in you:
       O Master, grant
       that I may never seek
       so much to be consoled
       as to console;
       to be understood
       as to understand,
       to be loved,
       as to love with all my soul!

2 Make me a channel of your peace:
   where there's despair in life
       let me bring hope,
   where there is darkness, only light,
   and where there's sadness, ever joy:
       O Master, grant . . .

3 Make me a channel of your peace:
   it is in pardoning that we are pardoned,
   in giving of ourselves that we receive,
   and in dying that we're born to eternal life.

193 © Paul Wigmore / Jubilate Hymns

1 Mary came with meekness,
   Jesus Christ to bear,
   laid the Lord of glory
   in a manger there.
       We come rejoicing,
       Jesus Christ to love:
       baby in a manger –
       king of heaven above!

2 Angels came with praises,
   Jesus Christ to name,
   heaven's choirs exalting
   him who bears our shame.
       We come rejoicing . . .

3 Shepherds came with trembling,
   Jesus Christ to see;
   king who, at their bidding,
   would their shepherd be.
       We come rejoicing . . .

4   Wise men came with treasure,
    Jesus Christ to bless –
    he who shares all blessings
    heaven and earth possess.
      We come rejoicing . . .

194   From Luke 1 (*Magnificat*)
© Michael Perry / Jubilate Hymns

1   Mary sang a song, a song of love,
    magnified the mighty Lord above;
    melodies of praise his name extol
    from the very depths of Mary's soul:

2   'God the Lord has done great things for me,
    looked upon my life's humility;
    happy they shall call me from this day –
    merciful is he whom we obey.

3   'To the humble soul our God is kind,
    to the proud he brings unease of mind.
    Who uplifts the poor, pulls down the strong?
    God alone has power to right the wrong!

4   'He who has been Israel's strength and stay
    fills the hungry, sends the rich away;
    God has shown his promise firm and sure,
    faithful to his people evermore.'

5   This was Mary's song as we recall,
    mother to the saviour of us all:
    magnify his name and sing his praise,
    worship and adore him, all your days!

195   Philipp Bliss

1   Man of sorrows! what a name
    for the Son of God, who came
    ruined sinners to reclaim:
      Alleluia! what a saviour!

2   Mocked by insults harsh and crude,
    in my place condemned he stood;
    sealed my pardon with his blood:
      Alleluia! what a saviour!

3   Guilty, helpless, lost were we:
    blameless Lamb of God was he,
    sacrificed to set us free:
      Alleluia! what a saviour!

4   Lifted up was he to die:
    'It is finished!' was his cry;
    now in heaven exalted high:
      Alleluia! what a saviour!

5   When he comes, our glorious king,
    all his ransomed home to bring;
    then again this song we'll sing:
      'Alleluia! what a saviour!'

196   From 2 Corinthians 13
John Newton

1   May the grace of Christ our saviour
    and the Father's boundless love,
    with the Holy Spirit's favour,
    rest upon us from above.

2   So may we remain in union
    with each other and the Lord,
    and possess, in sweet communion,
    joys which earth cannot afford.

197   Graham Kendrick
© 1986 Thankyou Music

1   Meekness and majesty,
    manhood and deity,
    in perfect harmony –
    the man who is God:
    Lord of eternity
    dwells in humanity,
    kneels in humility
    and washes our feet.
      Oh what a mystery –
      meekness and majesty:
      bow down and worship,
      for this is your God,
      this is your God!

2   Father's pure radiance,
    perfect in innocence,
    yet learns obedience
    to death on a cross:
    suffering to give us life,
    conquering through sacrifice –
    and, as they crucify,
    prays, 'Father, forgive'.
      O what a mystery . . .

3   Wisdom unsearchable,
    God the invisible,
    love indestructible
    in frailty appears:
    Lord of infinity,
    stooping so tenderly,
    lifts our humanity
    to the heights of his throne.
      O what a mystery . . .

198   Eleanor Farjeon
© David Higham Associates

1   Morning has broken like the first morning;
    blackbird has spoken like the first bird:
    praise for the singing, praise for the morning,
    praise for them springing
      fresh from the word!

2 Sweet the rain's new fall, sunlit from heaven,
like the first dew fall on the first grass:
praise for the sweetness of the wet garden,
sprung in completeness where his feet pass!

3 Mine is the sunlight, mine is the morning
born of the one light Eden saw play:
praise with elation, praise every morning,
God's re-creation of the new day!

199 Katie Wilkinson
© in this version Jubilate Hymns

1 May the mind of Christ my saviour
live in me from day to day,
by his love and power controlling
all I do and say.

2 May the word of God enrich me
with his truth, from hour to hour;
so that all may see I triumph
only through his power.

3 May the peace of God my Father
in my life for ever reign,
that I may be calm to comfort
those in grief and pain.

4 May the love of Jesus fill me
as the waters fill the sea,
him exalting, self abasing –
this is victory!

5 May his beauty rest upon me
as I seek to make him known;
so that all may look to Jesus,
seeing him alone.

200 Frederick Faber
© in this version Jubilate Hymns

1 My God, how wonderful you are,
your majesty how bright;
how beautiful your mercy-seat
in depths of burning light!

2 Creator from eternal years
and everlasting Lord,
by holy angels day and night
unceasingly adored,
unceasingly adored!

3 How wonderful, how beautiful
the sight of you must be –
your endless wisdom, boundless power,
and awesome purity!

4 O how I fear you, living God,
with deepest, tenderest fears,
and worship you with trembling hope
and penitential tears,
and penitential tears!

5 But I may love you too, O Lord,
though you are all-divine,
for you have stooped to ask of me
this feeble love of mine.

6 Father of Jesus, love's reward,
great king upon your throne,
what joy to see you as you are
and know as I am known,
and know as I am known!

7 My God, how wonderful you are,
your majesty, how bright;
how beautiful your mercy-seat
in depths of burning light!
My God, how wonderful you are!

201 Edward Mote
© in this version Jubilate Hymns

1 My hope is built on nothing less
than Jesus' blood and righteousness;
no merit of my own I claim,
but wholly trust in Jesus' name.
On Christ, the solid rock, I stand –
all other ground is sinking sand.

2 When weary in this earthly race,
I rest on his unchanging grace;
in every wild and stormy gale
my anchor holds and will not fail.
On Christ, the solid rock . . .

3 His vow, his covenant and blood
are my defence against the flood;
when earthly hopes are swept away
he will uphold me on that day.
On Christ, the solid rock . . .

4 When the last trumpet's voice shall sound,
O may I then in him be found!
clothed in his righteousness alone,
faultless to stand before his throne.
On Christ, the solid rock . . .

202 Josiah Condor

1 My Lord, I did not choose you
for that could never be;
my heart would still refuse you
had you not chosen me:
you took the sin that stained me,
you cleansed me, made me new,
for you, Lord, had ordained me
that I should live in you.

2 Unless your grace had called me
and taught my opening mind
the world would have enthralled me,
to heavenly glories blind:
my heart knows none above you;
for you I long, I thirst,
and know that, if I love you,
Lord, you have loved me first.

203
© Christopher Idle / Jubilate Hymns

1 My Lord of light who made the worlds,
in wisdom you have spoken;
but those who heard your wise commands
your holy law have broken.

2 My Lord of love who knew no sin,
a sinner's death enduring:
for us you wore a crown of thorns,
a crown of life securing.

3 My Lord of life who came in fire
when Christ was high ascended:
your burning love is now released,
our days of fear are ended.

4 My Lord of lords, one Trinity,
to your pure name be given
all glory now and evermore,
all praise in earth and heaven.

204
© Christopher Idle / Jubilate Hymns

1 My Lord, you wore no royal crown;
you did not wield the powers of state,
nor did you need a scholar's gown
or priestly robe, to make you great.

2 You never used a killer's sword
to end an unjust tyranny;
your only weapon was your word,
for truth alone could set us free.

3 You did not live a world away
in hermit's cell or desert cave,
but felt our pain and shared each day
with those you came to seek and save.

4 You made no mean or cunning move,
chose no unworthy compromise,
but carved a track of burning love
through tangles of deceit and lies.

5 You came unequalled, undeserved,
to be what I was meant to be;
to serve instead of being served,
to pay for my iniquity.

6 So when I stumble, set me right;
command my life as you require;
let all your gifts be my delight
and you, my Lord, my one desire.

205
Graham Kendrick
© 1989 Make Way Music

1 My Lord, what love is this
that pays so dearly:
that I, the guilty one
may go free!
    Amazing love, oh what sacrifice,
    the Son of God given for me!
    My debt he pays and my death he dies
    that I might live,
    that I might live.

2 And so, they watched him die
despised, rejected:
but oh, the blood he shed
flowed for me!
    Amazing love . . .

3 And now this love of Christ
shall flow like rivers:
come wash your guilt away,
live again!
    Amazing love . . .

206
Samuel Crossman
© in this version Jubilate Hymns

1 My song is love unknown,
my saviour's love for me;
love to the loveless shown
that they might lovely be:
but who am I, that for my sake
my Lord should take frail flesh and die?

2 He came from heaven's throne
salvation to bestow;
but men refused, and none
the longed-for Christ would know:
this is my friend, my friend indeed,
who at my need his life did spend.

3 Sometimes they crowd his way
and his sweet praises sing,
resounding all the day
hosannas to their king:
then 'crucify' is all their breath,
and for his death they thirst and cry.

4 Why, what has my Lord done
to cause this rage and spite?
he made the lame to run,
and gave the blind their sight:
what injuries! yet these are why
the Lord most high so cruelly dies.

5 With angry shouts, they have
  my dear Lord done away;
  a murderer they save,
  the prince of life they slay!
  yet willingly he bears the shame
  that through his name all may be free.

6 In life no house, no home,
  my Lord on earth may have;
  in death no friendly tomb
  but what a stranger gave.
  What may I say? Heaven was his home
  but mine the tomb in which he lay.

7 Here might I stay and sing
  of him my soul adores;
  never was love, dear King,
  never was grief like yours! –
  this is my friend in whose sweet praise
  I all my days could gladly spend.

One or more of verses 4, 5 and 6 may be omitted

207   © Timothy Dudley-Smith

1 Name of all majesty,
  fathomless mystery,
  king of the ages
  by angels adored;
      power and authority,
      splendour and dignity,
      bow to his mastery –
  Jesus is Lord!

2 Child of our destiny,
  God from eternity,
  love of the Father
  on sinners outpoured;
      see now what God has done
      sending his only Son,
      Christ the belovèd One –
  Jesus is Lord!

3 Saviour of Calvary,
  costliest victory,
  darkness defeated
  and Eden restored;
      born as a man to die,
      nailed to a cross on high,
      cold in the grave to lie –
  Jesus is Lord!

4 Source of all sovereignty,
  light, immortality,
  life everlasting
  and heaven assured;
      so with the ransomed, we
      praise him eternally,
      Christ in his majesty –
  Jesus is Lord!

208   John Keble

1 New every morning is the love
  our waking and uprising prove:
  through sleep and darkness safely brought,
  restored to life and power and thought.

2 New mercies, each returning day,
  surround your people as they pray:
  new dangers past, new sins forgiven,
  new thoughts of God, new hopes of heaven.

3 If in our daily life our mind
  be set to hallow all we find,
  new treasures still, of countless price,
  God will provide for sacrifice.

4 The trivial round, the common task,
  will give us all we ought to ask:
  room to deny ourselves, a road
  to bring us daily nearer God.

5 Prepare us, Lord, in your dear love
  for perfect rest with you above,
  and help us, this and every day,
  to grow more like you as we pray.

209   © Timothy Dudley-Smith

1 No weight of gold or silver
  can measure human worth;
  no soul secures its ransom
  with all the wealth of earth:
  no sinners find their freedom
  but by the gift unpriced,
  the Lamb of God unblemished,
  the precious blood of Christ.

2 Our sins, our griefs and troubles,
  he bore and made his own;
  we hid our faces from him,
  rejected and alone;
  his wounds are for our healing,
  our peace is by his pain:
  behold, the Man of sorrows,
  the Lamb for sinners slain!

3 In Christ the past is over,
  a new world now begins;
  with him we rise to freedom
  who saves us from our sins:
  we live by faith in Jesus
  to make his glory known:
  behold, the Man of sorrows,
  the Lamb upon his throne!

210

1 Not the grandeur of the mountains,
nor the splendour of the sea,
can excel the ceaseless wonder
of my Saviour's love to me:
    for his love to me is faithful,
    and his mercy is divine;
    and his truth is everlasting,
    and his perfect peace is mine.

2 Not the streams that fill the valleys,
nor the clouds that drift along,
can delight me more than Jesus
or replace my grateful song:
    for his love . . .

3 Yet these all convey his beauty
and proclaim his power and grace –
for they are among the tokens
of the love upon his face:
    for his love . . .

211

1 Now at last,
your servant can depart in peace,
for your word
is finally fulfilled.

2 My own eyes
have witnessed your salvation, Lord,
which is seen
throughout the whole wide world.

3 Light for all,
revealing you to every land.
Glorious sight –
your people Israel's hope,
your people Israel's hope,
your people Israel's hope.

212

1 Now let us learn of Christ:
he speaks, and we shall find
he lightens our dark mind;
so let us learn of Christ.

2 Now let us love in Christ
as he has first loved us;
as he endured the cross,
so let us love in Christ.

3 Now let us grow in Christ
and look to things above,
and speak the truth in love;
so let us grow in Christ.

4 Now let us stand in Christ
in every trial we meet,
in all his strength complete;
so let us stand in Christ.

213

1 Now thank we all our God
with hearts and hands and voices;
who wondrous things has done!
in whom this world rejoices;
who from our mothers' arms,
has blessed us on our way
with countless gifts of love,
and still is ours today.

2 So may this bounteous God
through all our life be near us;
with ever joyful hearts,
and heaven's peace to cheer us;
and keep us in his grace,
and guide us when perplexed,
and free us from all ills
in this world and the next.

3 All praise and thanks to God
who reigns in highest heaven;
to Father and to Son
and Spirit now be given:
to the eternal God,
whom heaven and earth adore,
the one who was, is now,
and shall be evermore.

214

1 O Breath of life, come sweeping through us,
revive your church with life and power;
O Breath of life, come, cleanse, renew us
and fit your church to meet this hour.

2 O Wind of God, come bend us, break us
till humbly we confess our need;
then, in your tenderness remake us,
revive, restore – for this we plead.

3 O Breath of love, come breathe within us,
renewing thought and will and heart;
come, love of Christ, afresh to win us,
revive your church in every part!

215

1 O come, all ye faithful,
joyful and triumphant;
O come ye, O come ye to Bethlehem;
come and behold him,
    born the king of angels!

O come, let us adore him,
O come, let us adore him,
O come, let us adore him,
Christ the Lord!

2 God from God,
Light from light –
lo, he abhors not the virgin's womb!
Very God, begotten, not created.
O come . . .

3 Sing, choirs of angels,
sing in exultation!
Sing, all ye citizens of heaven above,
'Glory to God in the highest!'
O come . . .

4 Yea, Lord, we greet thee
born for our salvation;
Jesus, to thee be glory given!
Word of the Father now in flesh appearing.
O come . . .

OR, ON CHRISTMAS DAY

4 Yea, Lord, we greet thee,
born this happy morning;
Jesus, to thee be glory given!
Word of the Father now in flesh appearing.
O come . . .

216 From the Latin
John Neale and others
© in this version Jubilate Hymns

1 O come, O come, Emmanuel
and ransom captive Israel
who mourns in lonely exile here
until the Son of God draws near:
    Rejoice, rejoice!
    Emmanuel shall come to you O Israel.

2 O come, true Branch of Jesse, free
your children from this tyranny;
from depths of hell your people save,
to rise victorious from the grave:
    Rejoice, rejoice . . .

3 O come, bright Daybreak, come and cheer
our spirits by your advent here;
dispel the long night's lingering gloom
and pierce the shadows of the tomb:
    Rejoice, rejoice . . .

4 O come, strong Key of David, come
and open wide our heavenly home;
make safe the way that leads on high
and close the path to misery:
    Rejoice, rejoice . . .

5 O come, O come, great Lord of might
who long ago on Sinai's height
gave all your tribes the ancient law
in cloud and majesty and awe:
    Rejoice, rejoice . . .

217 Charles Wesley

1 O for a heart to praise my God –
a heart from sin set free,
a heart that's sprinkled with the blood
so freely shed for me.

2 A heart resigned, submissive, meek,
my great redeemer's throne;
where only Christ is heard to speak,
where Jesus reigns alone.

3 A humble, lowly, contrite heart,
believing, true, and clean,
which neither life nor death can part
from him who dwells within.

4 A heart in every thought renewed,
and full of love divine;
perfect and right and pure and good –
your life revealed in mine.

5 Your nature gracious Lord, impart –
come quickly from above,
write your new name upon my heart,
your new best name of love!

218 Charles Wesley

1 O for a thousand tongues to sing
my great redeemer's praise,
the glories of my God and king,
the triumphs of his grace!

2 Jesus, the name that charms our fears
and bids our sorrows cease:
this music in the sinner's ears
is life and health and peace.

3 He breaks the power of cancelled sin,
he sets the prisoner free;
his blood can make the foulest clean,
his blood availed for me.

4 He speaks – and, listening to his voice,
new life the dead receive,
the mournful broken hearts rejoice,
the humble poor believe.

5 Hear him, you deaf! his praise, you dumb,
your loosened tongues employ;
you blind, now see your saviour come,
and leap, you lame, for joy!

6 My gracious Master and my God,
assist me to proclaim
and spread through all the earth abroad
the honours of your name.

219

© Michael Perry / Jubilate Hymns

1 O God beyond all praising,
we worship you today
and sing the love amazing
that songs cannot repay;
for we can only wonder
at every gift you send,
at blessings without number
and mercies without end:
we lift our hearts before you
and wait upon your word,
we honour and adore you,
our great and mighty Lord.

2 Then hear, O gracious Saviour,
accept the love we bring,
that we who know your favour
may serve you as our king;
and whether our tomorrows
be filled with good or ill,
we'll triumph through our sorrows
and rise to bless you still:
to marvel at your beauty
and glory in your ways,
and make a joyful duty
our sacrifice of praise!

220
Isaac Watts

1 O God, our help in ages past,
our hope for years to come,
our shelter from the stormy blast,
and our eternal home:

2 Beneath the shadow of your throne
your people lived secure;
sufficient is your arm alone,
and our defence is sure.

3 Before the hills in order stood,
or earth from darkness came,
from everlasting you are God,
to endless years the same.

4 A thousand ages in your sight
are like an evening gone;
short as the watch that ends the night,
before the rising sun.

5 Time, like an ever-rolling stream,
will bear us all away;
we pass forgotten, as a dream
dies with the dawning day.

6 O God, our help in ages past,
our hope for years to come:
be our defence while life shall last,
and our eternal home!

221
John Bode

1 O Jesus, I have promised
to serve you to the end –
be now and ever near me,
my Master and my Friend:
I shall not fear the battle
if you are by my side,
nor wander from the pathway
if you will be my guide.

2 O let me feel you near me –
the world is ever near;
I see the sights that dazzle,
the tempting sounds I hear;
my foes are ever near me,
around me and within:
but Jesus, draw still nearer
and shield my soul from sin!

3 O let me hear you speaking
in accents clear and still;
above the storms of passion,
the murmurs of self-will;
O speak to reassure me,
to hasten or control;
and speak to make me listen,
O Guardian of my soul.

4 O let me see your footmarks
and in them place my own:
my hope to follow truly
is in your strength alone.
O guide me, call me, draw me,
uphold me to the end;
and then in heaven receive me,
my Saviour and my Friend.

222
Phillips Brooks

1 O little town of Bethlehem,
how still we see you lie!
Above your deep and dreamless sleep
the silent stars go by:
yet in your dark streets shining
is everlasting light;
the hopes and fears of all the years
are met in you tonight.

2 For Christ is born of Mary
and, gathered all above
while mortals sleep, the angels keep
their watch of wondering love:
O morning stars, together
proclaim the holy birth,
and praises sing to God the king,
and peace to all the earth.

3 How silently, how silently
the wondrous gift is given!
So God imparts to human hearts
the blessings of his heaven:
no ear may hear his coming,
but in this world of sin,
where meek souls will receive him –
still the dear Christ enters in.

4 O holy child of Bethlehem,
descend to us, we pray;
cast out our sin and enter in,
be born in us today!
We hear the Christmas angels
the great glad tidings tell –
O come to us, abide with us,
our Lord Emmanuel.

223 From Psalm 22, John Bell and Graham Maule
© Wild Goose Publications / The Iona Community

ALL
O Lord my God, O Lord my God,
why do you seem so far from me,
O Lord my God?

GROUP / SOLO
1 Night and morning I make my prayer:
peace for this place, and help for there;
waiting and wondering,
waiting and wondering –
does God care; does God care?
ALL O Lord my God . . .

GROUP / SOLO
2 Pain and suffering unbound and blind
plague the progress of humankind,
always demanding,
always demanding –
does God mind; does God mind?
ALL O Lord my God . . .

GROUP / SOLO
3 Why, oh why do the wicked thrive,
poor folk perish, the rich survive;
begging the question,
begging the question –
is God alive; is God alive?
ALL O Lord my God . . .

GROUP / SOLO
4 Turn again as you hear my plea,
tend the torment in all I see;
loving and healing,
loving and healing –
set me free, set me free!
ALL O Lord my God . . .

224 Graham Kendrick
© 1987 Make Way Music

1 O Lord, the clouds are gathering,
the fire of judgement burns.
How we have fallen!
O Lord, you stand appalled to see
your laws of love so scorned,
and lives so broken.
A   Have mercy, Lord,
B   have mercy, Lord.
A   Forgive us, Lord,
B   forgive us, Lord.
ALL Restore us, Lord;
revive your church again.
A   Let justice flow,
B   let justice flow,
A   like rivers,
B   like rivers;
ALL and righteousness
like a never-failing stream.

2 O Lord, over the nations now,
where is the dove of peace?
Her wings are broken!
O Lord, while precious children starve,
the tools of war increase,
their bread is stolen.
A Have mercy, Lord . . .

3 O Lord, dark powers are poised
to flood our streets with hate and fear.
We must awaken!
O Lord, let love reclaim the lives
that sin would sweep away,
and let your kingdom come!
A Have mercy, Lord . . .

4 Yet, O Lord, your glorious cross
shall tower triumphant in this land,
evil confounding;
through the fire, your suffering church
display the glories of her Christ,
praises resounding.
A Have mercy, Lord . . .

The congregation may divide at A and B

225
From Psalm 90
© Basil Bridge

1 O Lord, the refuge of each generation,
  you reigned before the universe began;
  we bear your stamp,
       the marks of your creation,
  and yet how frail we are, how brief life's span!

2 One thousand years like yesterday in passing,
  our fleeting lives
       like half-remembered dreams,
  or weeds that flower at noon
       but die by evening –
  so, Lord, to you our transient glory seems.

3 O Holy Lord, forgive our self-deceiving –
  our secret sins are clear before your face:
  grant us release, the joy of those believing
  they are restored by your eternal grace.

4 Time rushes on: give us a heart of wisdom
  that seeks your will
       and follows your commands;
  show us your deeds,
       your glory to our children,
  work out your timeless purpose
       through our hands.

226
Charles Wesley
© in this version Jubilate Hymns

1 O Lord, who came from realms above
  the pure celestial fire to impart,
  kindle a flame of sacred love
  upon the altar of my heart.

2 There let it for your glory burn
  with inextinguishable blaze,
  and trembling to its source return
  in humble prayer and fervent praise.

3 Jesus, confirm my heart's desire
  to work and speak and think for you;
  still let me guard the holy fire,
  and still in me your gift renew.

4 Here let me prove your perfect will,
  my acts of faith and love repeat,
  till death your endless mercies seal
  and make the sacrifice complete!

227
After George Matheson
© in this version Word & Music / Jubilate Hymns

1 O love that will not let me go,
  revive your loveliness in me:
  I give you back the life I owe
  that in your ocean depths its flow
       may richer, fuller be.

2 O light that follows all my way,
  renew your radiance in me:
  I welcome your life-giving ray
  that in your sunshine's blaze each day
       may brighter, fairer be.

3 O joy that seeks for me through pain,
  restore your hopefulness to me;
  I trace the rainbow through the rain
  and trust your promise once again:
       that dawn shall tearless be.

*Could
old use
words
here*

4 O cross that raises up my head,
  remove the sinfulness from me:
  I lay in dust life's glory dead,
  and from the ground there blossoms red,
       life that shall endless be.

228
James Montgomery

1 O Spirit of the living God,
  in all the fulness of your grace,
  wherever human feet have trod,
  descend upon our fallen race:

2 Give tongues of fire and hearts of love
  to preach the reconciling word;
  anoint with power from heaven above
  whenever gospel truth is heard:

3 Let darkness turn to radiant light,
  confusion vanish from your path;
  those who are weak inspire with might:
  let mercy triumph over wrath!

4 O Spirit of our God, prepare
  the whole wide world the Lord to meet;
  breathe out new life, like morning air,
  till hearts of stone begin to beat:

5 Baptize the nations; far and near
  the triumphs of the cross record;
  till Christ in glory shall appear
  and every race declare him Lord!

229
© Michael Saward / Jubilate Hymns

1 O Trinity, O Trinity,
       the uncreated One;
  O Unity, O Unity,
       of Father, Spirit, Son:
  you are without beginning,
  your life is never ending;
       and though our tongues
       are earth bound clay,
  light them with flaming fire today.

2 O Majesty, O Majesty,
   the Father of our race;
   O Mystery, O Mystery,
   we cannot see your face:
   your justice is unswerving,
   your love is overpowering:
   and though our tongues
      are earth bound clay,
   light them with flaming fire today.

3 O Virgin-born, O Virgin-born,
   of humankind the least;
   O Victim torn, O Victim torn,
   both spotless lamb and priest:
   you died and rose victorious,
   you reign above all-glorious;
   and though . . .

4 O Wind of God, O Wind of God,
   invigorate the dead;
   O Fire of God, O Fire of God,
   your burning radiance spread:
   your fruit our lives renewing,
   your gifts, the church transforming;
   and though . . .

5 O Trinity, O Trinity,
   the uncreated One;
   O Unity, O Unity,
   of Father, Spirit, Son:
   you are without beginning,
   your life is never ending;
   and though . . .

230   After William Kethe
          Robert Grant

1 O worship the King all glorious above,
   and gratefully sing his power and his love,
   our shield and defender, the Ancient of Days,
   pavilioned in splendour
      and girded with praise.

2 O tell of his might and sing of his grace,
   whose robe is the light, whose canopy space;
   his chariots of wrath
      the deep thunder-clouds form,
   and dark is his path on the wings of the storm.

3 The earth, with its store of wonders untold,
   Almighty, your power has founded of old,
   established it fast by a changeless decree,
   and round it has cast like a garment the sea.

4 Your bountiful care what tongue can recite?
   it breathes in the air, it shines in the light;
   it streams from the hills,
      it descends to the plain,
   and sweetly distils in the dew and the rain.

5 We children of dust are feeble and frail –
   in you we will trust, for you never fail;
   your mercies how tender,
      how firm to the end!
   our maker, defender, redeemer and friend.

6 O measureless Might, unchangeable Love,
   whom angels delight to worship above!
   your ransomed creation with glory ablaze,
   in true adoration shall sing to your praise!

231   John Monsell

1 O worship the Lord in the beauty of holiness,
   bow down before him, his glory proclaim;
   with gold of obedience
      and incense of lowliness,
   kneel and adore him – the Lord is his name.

2 Low at his feet
      lay your burden of carefulness,
   high on his heart he will bear it for you,
   comfort your sorrows
      and answer your prayerfulness,
   guiding your steps in the way that is true.

3 Fear not to enter his courts in the slenderness
   of the poor wealth
      you would count as your own;
   truth in its beauty and love in its tenderness –
   these are the offerings to bring to his throne.

4 These, though we bring them
      in trembling and fearfulness,
   he will accept for the Name that is dear;
   mornings of joy
      give for evenings of tearfulness,
   trust for our trembling and hope for our fear.

5 O worship the Lord in the beauty of holiness,
   bow down before him, his glory proclaim;
   with gold of obedience
      and incense of lowliness,
   kneel and adore him – the Lord is his name.

232   Cecil Alexander

1 Once in royal David's city
   stood a lowly cattle shed,
   where a mother laid her baby
   in a manger for his bed:
   Mary was that mother mild,
   Jesus Christ, her little child.

2 He came down to earth from heaven
  who is God and Lord of all;
  and his shelter was a stable
  and his cradle was a stall:
  with the poor and meek and lowly
  lived on earth our saviour holy.

3 And through all his wondrous childhood
  he would honour and obey,
  love and watch the gentle mother
  in whose tender arms he lay:
  Christian children all should be
  kind, obedient, good as he.

4 For he is our childhood's pattern:
  day by day like us he grew;
  he was little, weak and helpless –
  tears and smiles like us he knew:
  and he feels for all our sadness,
  and he shares in all our gladness.

5 And our eyes at last shall see him,
  through his own redeeming love;
  for that child, so dear and gentle,
  is our Lord in heaven above:
  and he leads his children on
  to the place where he has gone.

6 Not in that poor lowly stable
  with the oxen standing by,
  we shall see him, but in heaven,
  set at God's right hand on high:
  there his children gather round
  bright like stars, with glory crowned.

Verse 3 may be omitted

233   For Church Pastoral Aid Society
© Michael Perry / Jubilate Hymns

1 One thing I know, that Christ has healed me –
  though I was blind, yet now I see;
  to him I owe, whose love has sealed me,
  my heart and mind at last set free.

2 One thing I pray – that in my weakness,
  God's perfect might will make me strong;
  learning Christ's way whose selfless meekness
  is my delight, my peace, my song.

3 One thing I do – put sin behind me,
  press for the goal to win the prize;
  for Christ I go who came to find me,
  making me whole to gain the skies.

4 One faith, one Lord, one new creation,
  one hope of our eternity!
  One holy God! To our salvation,
  glory and power for ever be!

234   © Michael Saward / Jubilate Hymns

1 'Peace be with you all,' we sing;
  peace from Christ, our Lord and king,
  he it is who makes us one,
  God's eternal rising Son.

2 Bound together in his name,
  welded by the Spirit's flame;
  at his table here we kneel
  and his living presence feel.

3 Bread is broken for our food;
  wine we share in gratitude.
  His flesh and blood he gave
  for the world he died to save.

4 So with empty hands, we bow
  to receive our saviour now
  and, renewed in mind and heart,
  in the peace of Christ depart.

235   After Thomas Ken
© in this version Jubilate Hymns

Praise God from whom all blessings flow,
in heaven above and earth below:
one God, three persons, we adore –
to him be praise for evermore!

236   From Psalm 148
© Michael Perry / Jubilate Hymns

1 Praise him, praise him, praise him,
      powers and dominations;
  praise his name in glorious light,
      you creatures of the day:
  moon and stars ring praises
      through the constellations –
  Lord God, whose word
      shall never pass away.

2 Praise him, praise him, praise him,
      ocean depths and waters;
  elements of earth and heaven,
      your several praises blend:
  birds and beasts and cattle,
      Adam's sons and daughters,
  worship the king
      whose reign shall never end!

3 Praise him, praise him, praise him,
      saints of God who fear him;
  to the highest name of all,
      concerted anthems raise,
  all you seed of Israel,
      holy people near him
  whom he exalts to power
      and crowns with praise!

237
From Psalm 103
Henry Francis Lyte

1 Praise my soul, the king of heaven;
   to his feet your tribute bring!
   Ransomed, healed, restored, forgiven,
   who like me his praise should sing?
       Alleluia, alleluia!
   praise the everlasting king!

2 Praise him for his grace and favour
   to our fathers in distress;
   praise him still the same as ever,
   slow to blame and swift to bless,
       Alleluia, alleluia!
   glorious in his faithfulness!

3 Father-like, he tends and spares us;
   all our hopes and fears he knows,
   in his hands he gently bears us,
   rescues us from all our foes,
       Alleluia, alleluia!
   widely as his mercy flows.

4 Angels, help us to adore him –
   you behold him face to face;
   sun and moon, bow down before him,
   praise him, all in time and space,
       Alleluia, alleluia!
   praise with us the God of grace!

238
From Psalm 66
© Christopher Idle / Jubilate Hymns

1 Praise our God with shouts of joy,
   sing the glory of his name;
   join to lift his praises high,
   through the world his love proclaim.

2 Come and see what God has done
   by the power of his right hand;
   see the battles he has won
   by his word of swift command.

3 God has tamed the raging seas,
   carved a highway through the tide,
   paid the cost of our release,
   come himself to be our guide.

4 God has put us to the test,
   bringing us through flood and fire
   into freedom, peace and rest,
   for our good is his desire.

5 God has not despised my prayer
   nor kept back his love for me;
   he has raised me from despair –
   to our God all glory be!

6 Praise our God with shouts of joy,
   sing the glory of his name;
   join to lift his praises high,
   through the world his love proclaim.

239
From Psalm 148
© Timothy Dudley-Smith

1 Praise the Lord of heaven,
   praise him in the height;
   praise him, all his angels,
   praise him, hosts of light.
   Sun and moon together,
   shining stars aflame,
   planets in their courses,
   magnify his name –
   O magnify his name!

2 Earth and ocean praise him;
   mountains, hills and trees;
   fire and hail and tempest,
   wind and storm and seas.
   Praise him, fields and forests,
   birds on flashing wings,
   praise him, beasts and cattle,
   all created things –
   yes, all created things!

3 Now by prince and people
   let his praise be told;
   praise him, men and maidens,
   praise him, young and old.
   He, the Lord of glory!
   We, his praise proclaim!
   High above all heavens
   magnify his name –
   O magnify his name!

240
From Psalm 148
Foundling Hospital Collection

1 Praise the Lord, you heavens, adore him –
   praise him, angels in the height!
   Sun and moon, rejoice before him;
   praise him, all you stars and light!
   Praise the Lord, for he has spoken,
   worlds his mighty voice obeyed;
   laws which never shall be broken
   for their guidance he has made.

2 Praise the Lord, for he is glorious,
   never shall his promise fail:
   God has made his saints victorious,
   sin and death shall not prevail.
   Praise the God of our salvation!
   Hosts on high, his power proclaim;
   heaven and earth and all creation
   praise and glorify his name!

241
John Newman

1 Praise to the Holiest in the height,
and in the depth be praise;
in all his words most wonderful,
most sure in all his ways!

2 Oh loving wisdom of our God!
when all was sin and shame,
a second Adam to the fight
and to the rescue came.

3 Oh wisest love! that flesh and blood,
which did in Adam fail,
should strive afresh against the foe,
should strive and should prevail;

4 And that the highest gift of grace
should flesh and blood refine:
God's presence and his very self,
and essence all-divine.

5 Oh generous love! that he who came
as man to smite our foe,
the double agony for us
as man should undergo:

6 And in the garden secretly,
and on the cross on high,
should teach his brethren, and inspire
to suffer and to die.

7 Praise to the Holiest in the height,
and in the depth be praise;
in all his words most wonderful,
most sure in all his ways!

242
From Psalm 103
Catherine Winkworth and others

1 Praise to the Lord, the almighty,
the king of creation!
O my soul, praise him,
for he is your health and salvation!
Come, all who hear;
brothers and sisters, draw near,
praise him in glad adoration!

2 Praise to the Lord,
above all things so mightily reigning;
keeping us safe at his side,
and so gently sustaining.
Have you not seen
all you have needed has been
met by his gracious ordaining?

3 Praise to the Lord,
who shall prosper our work and defend us;
surely his goodness and mercy
shall daily attend us.
Ponder anew
what the almighty can do,
who with his love will befriend us.

4 Praise to the Lord –
O let all that is in me adore him!
All that has life and breath,
come now with praises before him!
Let the 'Amen!'
sound from his people again –
gladly we praise and adore him!

243
Fred Kaan
© Oxford University Press

1 Put peace into each other's hands
and like a treasure hold it,
protect it like a candle-flame,
with tenderness enfold it.

2 Put peace into each other's hands
with loving expectation;
be gentle in your words and ways,
in touch with God's creation.

3 Put peace into each other's hands,
like bread we break for sharing;
look people warmly in the eye:
our life is meant for caring.

4 As at communion, shape your hands
into a waiting cradle;
the gift of Christ receive, revere,
united round the table.

5 Put Christ into each other's hands:
he is love's deepest measure;
in love make peace, give peace a chance
and share it like a treasure.

244
Graham Kendrick
© 1983 Thankyou Music

Rejoice, rejoice! Christ is in you –
the hope of glory in our hearts.
He lives, he lives!
his breath is in you.
Arise! A mighty army we arise!

1 Now is the time for us to march
        upon the land –
into our hands
        he will give the ground we claim;
he rides in majesty to lead us into victory,
the world shall see that Christ is Lord.
        Rejoice, rejoice! Christ is in you –
        the hope of glory in our hearts.
        He lives, he lives!
        his breath is in you.
        Arise! A mighty army we arise!

2 God is at work in us his purpose to perform –
building a kingdom of power not of words;
where things impossible
        by faith shall be made possible:
let's give the glory to him now.
        Rejoice . . .

3 Though we are weak,
        his grace is everything we need –
we're made of clay, but this treasure is within;
he turns our weaknesses
        into his opportunities,
so that the glory goes to him.
        Rejoice . . .
        We arise! We arise! We arise!

245   Charles Wesley

1 Rejoice, the Lord is king!
Your Lord and king adore –
mortals, give thanks and sing,
and triumph evermore:
        lift up your heart, lift up your voice:
        rejoice! – again I say, rejoice!

2 Jesus, the saviour, reigns,
the God of truth and love;
when he had purged our stains
he took his seat above.
        lift up your heart . . .

3 His kingdom cannot fail,
he rules both earth and heaven;
the keys of death and hell
to Jesus now are given.
        lift up your heart . . .

4 He sits at God's right hand,
till all his foes submit
and bow to his command
and fall beneath his feet.
        lift up your heart . . .

5 Rejoice in glorious hope!
Jesus the judge shall come
and take his servants up
to their eternal home:
        we soon shall hear the archangel's voice:
        the trumpet sounds – rejoice, rejoice!

246   From Psalm 25
Chorus: © 1981 Paul Inwood / St Thomas More Group
Verses: © The Grail / A P Watt Ltd

Remember, remember your mercy, Lord;
remember, remember your mercy, Lord:
hear your people's prayer
        as they call to you;
remember, remember your mercy, Lord.

1 SOLO
Lord, make me know your ways,
Lord, teach me your paths;
make me walk in your truth, and teach me,
for you are God my saviour.
        ALL Remember, remember your mercy . . .

2 SOLO
Remember your mercy, Lord,
and the love you have shown from of old;
do not remember the sins of my youth.
        In your love remember me,
        in your love remember me
because of your goodness, O Lord.
        ALL Remember, remember your mercy . . .

3 SOLO
The Lord is good and upright,
he shows the path to all who stray;
he guides the humble in the right path,
he teaches his way to the poor.
        ALL Remember, remember your mercy . . .

247   Graham Kendrick
© 1981 Thankyou Music

1 Restore, O Lord,
the honour of your name
in works of sovereign power;
come shake the earth again
that all may see,
and come with reverent fears
to the living God
whose Kingdom shall outlast the years.

2 Restore, O Lord,
in all the earth your fame,
and in our time revive
the Church that bears your name;
and in your anger,
Lord, remember mercy –
O Living God,
whose mercy shall outlast the years.

3 Bend us, O Lord,
   where we are hard and cold,
   in your refiner's fire;
   come purify the gold:
   though suffering comes,
   and evil crouches near,
   still our living God
   is reigning – he is reigning here!

4 Restore, O Lord,
   the honour of your name
   in works of sovereign power;
   come shake the earth again
   that all may see,
   and come with reverent fears
   to the living God
   whose Kingdom shall outlast the years.

248 Albert Midlane
         © in this version Jubilate Hymns

1 Revive your church, O Lord,
   in grace and power draw near;
   speak with the voice that wakes the dead,
   and make your people hear!

2 Revive your church, O Lord,
   disturb the sleep of death;
   give life to smouldering embers now
   by your almighty breath.

3 Revive your church, O Lord,
   exalt your precious name;
   and by your Holy Spirit come
   and set our love aflame.

4 Revive your church, O Lord,
   give us a thirst for you,
   a hunger for the bread of life
   our spirits to renew.

5 Revive your church, O Lord,
   and let your power be shown;
   the gifts and graces shall be ours,
   the glory yours alone!

249 Henry Milman
         © in this version Jubilate Hymns

1 Ride on, ride on in majesty
   as all the crowds 'Hosanna!' cry;
   through waving branches slowly ride,
   O Saviour, to be crucified.

2 Ride on, ride on in majesty,
   in lowly pomp ride on to die;
   O Christ, your triumph now begin
   with captured death, and conquered sin!

3 Ride on, ride on in majesty:
   the angel armies of the sky
   look down with sad and wondering eyes
   to see the approaching sacrifice.

4 Ride on, ride on in majesty,
   the last and fiercest foe defy:
   the Father on his sapphire throne
   awaits his own anointed Son.

5 Ride on, ride on in majesty,
   in lowly pomp ride on to die;
   bow your meek head to mortal pain,
   then take, O God, your power and reign!

250 Augustus Toplady
         © in this version Jubilate Hymns

1 Rock of ages, cleft for me,
   hide me now, my refuge be;
   let the water and the blood
   from your wounded side which flowed,
   be for sin the double cure –
   cleanse me from its guilt and power.

2 Not the labours of my hands
   can fulfil your law's demands;
   could my zeal no respite know,
   could my tears for ever flow,
   all for sin could not atone:
   you must save and you alone.

3 Nothing in my hand I bring,
   simply to your cross I cling;
   naked, come to you for dress,
   helpless, look to you for grace;
   stained by sin, to you I cry:
   'Wash me, Saviour, or I die!'

4 While I draw this fleeting breath,
   when my eyelids close in death,
   when I soar through realms unknown,
   bow before the judgement throne:
   hide me then, my refuge be,
   Rock of ages, cleft for me.

251 From Psalm 91
         © Timothy Dudley-Smith

1 Safe in the shadow of the Lord,
   beneath his hand and power,
       I trust in him,
       I trust in him,
   my fortress and my tower.

2 My hope is set on God alone
   though Satan spreads his snare;
       I trust in him,
       I trust in him
   to keep me in his care.

3 A
From fears and phantoms of the night,
from foes about my way,
   I trust in him,
   I trust in him
by darkness as by day.

4 B
His holy angels keep my feet
secure from every stone;
   I trust in him,
   I trust in him,
and unafraid go on.

5 ALL
Strong in the everlasting name,
and in my Father's care,
   I trust in him,
   I trust in him,
who hears and answers prayer.

6 Safe in the shadow of the Lord,
possessed by love divine,
   I trust in him,
   I trust in him,
and meet his love with mine.

The congregation may divide at A and B

252   Edward Caswall
        © in this version Jubilate Hymns

1 See, amid the winter snow,
born for us on earth below;
see, the gentle Lamb appears,
promised from eternal years.
   Hail, O ever-blessèd morn:
   hail, redemption's happy dawn!
   Sing through all Jerusalem:
   'Christ is born in Bethlehem!'

2 Low within a manger lies
he who built the starry skies;
he who, throned in height sublime,
reigns above the cherubim.
   Hail, O ever-blessèd morn . . .

3 A
Say, you humble shepherds, say
what your joyful news today?
Tell us why you left your sheep
on the lonely mountain steep.
   Hail, O ever-blessèd morn . . .

4 B
'As we watched at dead of night,
all around us shone a light;
angels singing Peace on earth
told us of a Saviour's birth.'
   Hail, O ever-blessèd morn . . .

5 Sacred infant, king most dear,
what a tender love was here,
thus to come from highest bliss
down to such a world as this!
   Hail, O ever-blessèd morn . . .

6 Holy Saviour, born on earth,
teach us by your lowly birth;
grant that we may ever be
taught by such humility.
   Hail, O ever-blessèd morn . . .

The congregation may divide at A and B

253   © Michael Perry / Jubilate Hymns

1 See him lying on a bed of straw:
a draughty stable with an open door;
Mary cradling the babe she bore –
the prince of glory is his name.
   O now carry me to Bethlehem
   to see the Lord of love again:
   just as poor as was the stable then,
   the prince of glory when he came!

2 Star of silver, sweep across the skies,
show where Jesus in the manger lies;
shepherds, swiftly from your stupor rise
to see the saviour of the world!
   O now carry me . . .

3 Angels, sing again the song you sang,
sing the glory of God's gracious plan;
sing that Bethlehem's little baby can
be the saviour of us all.
   O now carry me . . .

4 Mine are riches, from your poverty,
from your innocence, eternity;
mine forgiveness by your death for me,
child of sorrow for my joy.
   O now carry me . . .

254   From the Latin, George Caird
        © Mrs V M Caird

1 Shepherds came, their praises bringing,
who had heard the angels singing:
'Far from you be fear unruly,
Christ is king of glory born.'

2 Wise men whom a star had guided
incense, gold and myrrh provided,
made their sacrifices truly
to the king of glory born.

3 Jesus born the king of heaven,
Christ to us through Mary given,
to your praise and honour duly
be resounding glory done.

255 After Joseph Möhr
John Young

1 Silent night! Holy night!
All is calm, all is bright
round the virgin and her child.
Holy infant, so gentle and mild,
   sleep in heavenly peace;
   sleep in heavenly peace!

2 Silent night! Holy night!
Shepherds quail at the sight,
glory streams from heaven afar;
heavenly hosts sing, 'Alleluia,
   Christ the saviour is born,
   Christ the saviour is born.'

3 Silent night! Holy night!
Son of God, love's pure light:
radiant beams your holy face
with the dawn of saving grace,
   Jesus, Lord, at your birth,
   Jesus, Lord, at your birth.

256 © Ernest Sands / St Thomas More Group

1 Sing of the Lord's goodness,
Father of all wisdom,
come to him and bless his name.
Mercy he has shown us,
his love is for ever,
faithful to the end of days.
   Come then, all you nations,
   sing of your Lord's goodness,
   melodies of praise and thanks to God;
   ring out the Lord's glory,
   praise him with your music,
   worship him and bless his name.

2 Power he has wielded,
honour is his garment,
risen from the snares of death.
His word he has spoken,
one bread he has broken,
new life he now gives to all.
   Come then . . .

3 Courage in our darkness,
comfort in our sorrow –
Spirit of our God most high!
Solace for the weary,
pardon for the sinner,
splendour of the living God!
   Come then . . .

4 Praise him with your singing,
praise him with the trumpet,
praise God with the lute and harp.
Praise him with the cymbals,
praise him with your dancing,
praise God till the end of days.
   Come then . . .

257 From Psalms 148, 150
Henry Baker
© in this version Jubilate Hymns

1 Sing praise to the Lord!
   Praise him in the height,
rejoice in his word you angels of light;
you heavens, adore him
   by whom you were made,
and worship before him in brightness arrayed.

2 Sing praise to the Lord!
   Praise him upon earth
in tuneful accord, you saints of new birth;
praise him who has brought you
   his grace from above,
praise him who has taught you
   to sing of his love.

3 Sing praise to the Lord!
   All things that give sound,
each jubilant chord re-echo around;
loud organs, his glory proclaim in deep tone,
and sweet harp, the story of what he has done.

4 Sing praise to the Lord!
   Thanksgiving and song
to him be outpoured all ages along;
for love in creation, for heaven restored,
for grace of salvation, sing praise to the Lord!

258 Charles Wesley

1 Soldiers of Christ, arise
and put your armour on;
strong in the strength which God supplies
through his eternal Son.
Strong in the Lord of hosts,
and in his mighty power;
who in the strength of Jesus trusts
is more than conqueror.

2 Stand then in his great might,
with all his strength endued;
and take, to arm you for the fight,
the weapons of our God.
To keep your armour bright
attend with constant care,
still walking in your captain's sight
and keeping watch with prayer.

3 From strength to strength go on:
   wrestle and fight and pray;
   tread all the powers of darkness down
   and win the well-fought day:
   Till, having all things done
   and all your conflicts past,
   you overcome through Christ alone
   and stand complete at last.

259
James Montogmery

1 Songs of praise the angels sang,
   heaven with alleluias rang
   when creation was begun;
   when God spoke, and it was done.

2 Songs of praise announced the dawn
   when the Prince of peace was born;
   songs of praise arose when he
   captive led captivity.

3 Heaven and earth must pass away –
   songs of praise shall crown that day!
   God will make new heavens and earth –
   songs of praise shall greet their birth!

4 And must we alone be dumb
   till that glorious kingdom come?
   No! the church delights to raise
   psalms and hymns and song of praise.

5 Saints below, with heart and voice
   still in songs of praise rejoice;
   learning here by faith and love
   songs of praise to sing above.

6 Hymns of glory, songs of praise,
   Father, now to you we raise;
   Saviour, Jesus, risen Lord,
   with the Spirit be adored.

260
Emily Crawford
© in this version Jubilate Hymns

1 Speak, Lord, in the stillness,
   speak your word to me;
   help me now to listen
   in expectancy.

2 Speak, O gracious Master,
   in this quiet hour;
   let me see your face, Lord,
   feel your touch of power.

3 For the words you give me,
   they are life indeed:
   living Bread from heaven,
   now my spirit feed.

4 Speak, your servant listens –
   I await your word;
   let me know your presence,
   let your voice be heard!

5 Fill me with the knowledge
   of your glorious will;
   all your own good pleasure
   in my life fulfil.

261
Andrew Reed
© in this version Jubilate Hymns

1 Spirit divine, inspire our prayers,
   and make our hearts your home;
   descend with all your gracious powers –
   O come, great Spirit, come!

2 Come as the light; reveal our need,
   our hidden failings show,
   and lead us in those paths of life
   in which the righteous go.

3 Come as the fire, and cleanse our hearts
   with purifying flame;
   let our whole life an offering be
   to our redeemer's name.

4 Come as the dew and gently bless
   this consecrated hour;
   may barren souls rejoice to know
   your life-creating power.

5 Come as the dove, and spread your wings,
   the wings of peaceful love;
   and let your church on earth become
   blessed as the church above.

6 Come as the wind with rushing sound
   and pentecostal grace,
   that all the world with joy may see
   the glory of your face.

262
From Isaiah 25
© Christopher Idle / Jubilate Hymns

1 See the feast our God prepares;
   all who hunger, come to dine!
   Jesus with his people shares
   richest food and finest wine.

2 Here he suddenly removes
   prisoners' shame and mourners' grief;
   here the wanderers whom he loves
   find their rest and their relief.

3 Now our tears are wiped away,
   now for ever death undone;
   he who rose on Easter Day
   ends our darkness like the sun.

4 Christ our God! With joy acclaim
all the glories of our king.
Christ the Lord! We love his name:
every tongue, his praises sing!

263 © Timothy Dudley-Smith

1 Spirit of faith, by faith be mine;
Spirit of truth, in wisdom shine;
Spirit of holiness divine,
    Spirit of Jesus, come!

2 Come to our hearts and there remain;
Spirit of life, our life sustain;
Spirit of grace and glory, reign!
    Spirit of Jesus, come!

264 © David Mowbray / Jubilate Hymns

1 Spirit of God most high,
Lord of all power and might;
source of our Easter joy,
well-spring of life and light:
    strip from the church its cloak of pride,
    a stumbling-block to those outside.

2 Wind of God's Spirit, blow!
into the valley sweep,
bringing dry bones to life,
wakening each from sleep:
    speak to the church your firm command,
    and bid a scattered army stand.

3 Fire of God's Spirit, melt
every unbending heart;
your people's love renew
as at their journey's start:
    your reconciling grace release
    to bring the Christian family peace.

4 Spirit of Christ our Lord,
send us to do your will;
nothing need hold us back
for you are with us still:
    forgetful of ourselves, may we
    receive your gift of unity!

265 Graham Kendrick
© 1988 Make Way Music

1 Such love, pure as the whitest snow,
such love weeps for the shame I know,
such love, paying the debt I owe –
    O Jesus, such love!

2 Such love, stilling my restlessness,
such love, filling my emptiness,
such love, showing me holiness –
    O Jesus, such love!

3 Such love springs from eternity,
such love, streaming through history,
such love, fountain of life to me:
    O Jesus, such love!

266 Frances Havergal
© in this version Jubilate Hymns

1 Take my life and let it be
all you purpose, Lord, for me;
consecrate my passing days,
let them flow in ceaseless praise.

2 Take my hands, and let them move
at the impulse of your love;
take my feet, and let them run
with the news of victory won.

3 Take my voice, and let me sing
always, only, for my King;
take my lips, let them proclaim
all the beauty of your name.

4 Take my wealth – all I possess,
make me rich in faithfulness;
take my mind that I may use
every power as you shall choose.

5 Take my motives and my will,
all your purpose to fulfil;
take my heart – it is your own,
it shall be your royal throne.

6 Take my love – my Lord, I pour
at your feet its treasure-store;
take myself, and I will be
yours for all eternity.

267 James Seddon
© Mrs M Seddon / Jubilate Hymns

1 Tell all the world of Jesus,
our saviour, Lord and king;
and let the whole creation
of his salvation sing:
proclaim his glorious greatness
in nature and in grace;
creator and redeemer,
the Lord of time and space.

2 Tell all the world of Jesus,
that everyone may find
the joy of his forgiveness –
true peace of heart and mind:
proclaim his perfect goodness,
his deep, unfailing care;
his love so rich in mercy,
a love beyond compare.

3 Tell all the world of Jesus,
that everyone may know
of his almighty triumph
defeating every foe:
proclaim his coming glory,
when sin is overthrown,
and he shall reign in splendour –
the King upon his throne!

268
From Luke 1
© Timothy Dudley-Smith

1 Tell out, my soul, the greatness of the Lord!
unnumbered blessings give my spirit voice;
tender to me the promise of his word;
in God my saviour shall my heart rejoice.

2 Tell out, my soul, the greatness of his name!
make known his might,
     the deeds his arm has done;
his mercy sure, from age to age the same;
his holy name – the Lord, the mighty one.

3 Tell out, my soul, the greatness of his might!
powers and dominions lay their glory by.
Proud hearts and stubborn wills
     are put to flight,
the hungry fed, the humble lifted high.

4 Tell out, my soul, the glories of his word!
firm is his promise, and his mercy sure.
Tell out, my soul, the greatness of the Lord
to children's children and for evermore!

269
John Ellerton
© in this version Jubilate Hymns

1 The day you gave us, Lord, is ended,
the darkness falls at your behest;
to you our morning hymns ascended,
your praise shall sanctify our rest.

2 We thank you that your church, unsleeping
while earth rolls onward into light,
through all the world her watch is keeping
and rests not now by day or night.

3 As to each continent and island
the dawn proclaims another day,
the voice of prayer is never silent,
nor dies the sound of praise away.

4 The sun that bids us rest is waking
your church beneath the western sky;
fresh voices hour by hour are making
your mighty deeds resound on high.

5 So be it, Lord: your throne shall never,
like earth's proud empires, pass away;
your kingdom stands, and grows for ever,
till all your works your rule obey.

270
John Daniels and Phil Johnson
© 1986 HarperCollins*Religious*

1 The earth was dark until you spoke –
then all was light and all was peace;
yet still, O God, so many wait
to see the flame of love released.
     Lights to the world!
     O Light divine,
     kindle in us a mighty flame,
     till every heart, consumed by love
     shall rise to praise
     your holy name!

2 In Christ you gave your gift of life
to save us from the depths of night:
O come and set our spirits free
and draw us to your perfect light!
     Lights to the world . . .

3 Where there is fear may we bring joy,
and healing to a world of pain:
Lord, build your kingdom through our lives
till Jesus walks this earth again.
     Lights to the world . . .

4 O burn in us, that we may burn
with love that triumphs in despair;
and touch our lives with such a fire
that souls may search and find you there.
     Lights to the world . . .

271
Unknown
© in this version Word & Music / Jubilate Hymns

1 The first nowell the angel did say,
was to Bethlehem's shepherds
     in fields as they lay;
in fields where they lay keeping their sheep
on a cold winter's night that was so deep:
     Nowell, nowell, nowell, nowell,
     born is the king of Israel!

2 The wise men from a country far
looked up and saw a guiding star;
they travelled on by night and day
to reach the place where Jesus lay:
     Nowell, nowell . . .

3 At Bethlehem they entered in,
on bended knee they worshipped him;
they offered there in his presence
their gold and myrrh and frankincense:
Nowell, nowell . . .

4 Then let us all with one accord
sing praises to our heavenly Lord;
for Christ has our salvation wrought
and with his blood our life has bought:
Nowell, nowell . . .

272 © Michael Perry / Jubilate Hymns

1 The hands of Christ, the caring hands,
they nailed them to a cross of wood;
the feet that climbed the desert road
and brought the news of peace with God,
they pierced them through.

2 The kingly Christ, the saviour-king,
they hailed him with a cruel crown;
the lips that spoke the truth alone,
that made the way to heaven known,
they mocked with wine.

3 Too late for life, in death too late
they tried to maim him with a spear;
for sacrilege they could not bear –
the sabbath comes, so they must tear
the heart from God.

4 To him be praise, all praise to him
who died upon the cross of pain;
whose agonies were not in vain –
for Christ the Lord is risen again
and brings us joy!

273 Thomas Kelly

1 The head that once was crowned with thorns
is crowned with glory now;
a royal diadem adorns
the mighty victor's brow.

2 The highest place that heaven affords
is his, is his by right;
the King of kings and Lord of lords
and heaven's eternal light.

3 The joy of all who dwell above,
the joy of all below –
to whom he demonstrates his love
and grants his name to know:

4 To them the cross with all its shame,
with all its grace is given;
their name, an everlasting name,
their joy, the joy of heaven.

5 They suffer with their Lord below,
they reign with him above;
their profit and their joy to know
the mystery of his love.

6 The cross he bore is life and health,
though shame and death to him;
his people's hope, his people's wealth,
their everlasting theme.

274 From Psalm 23, Henry Baker
© in this version Jubilate Hymns

1 The king of love my shepherd is,
whose goodness fails me never;
I nothing lack if I am his
and he is mine for ever.

2 Where streams of living water flow
a ransomed soul, he leads me;
and where the fertile pastures grow,
with food from heaven feeds me.

3 Perverse and foolish I have strayed,
but in his love he sought me;
and on his shoulder gently laid,
and home, rejoicing, brought me.

4 In death's dark vale I fear no ill
with you, dear Lord, beside me;
your rod and staff my comfort still,
your cross before to guide me.

5 You spread a banquet in my sight
of love beyond all knowing;
and oh the wonder and delight
from your pure chalice flowing!

6 And so through all the length of days
your goodness fails me never:
Good Shepherd, may I sing your praise
within your house for ever!

275 Bryn Rees
© Mrs M Rees

1 The kingdom of God is justice and joy;
for Jesus restores what sin would destroy.
God's power and glory in Jesus we know;
and here and hereafter
the kingdom shall grow.

2 The kingdom of God is mercy and grace;
the captives are freed, the sinners find place,
the outcast are welcomed
God's banquet to share;
and hope is awakened in place of despair.

3 The kingdom of God is challenge and choice:
  believe the good news, repent and rejoice!
  His love for us sinners
      brought Christ to his cross:
  our crisis of judgement for gain or for loss.

4 God's kingdom is come, the gift and the goal;
  in Jesus begun, in heaven made whole.
  The heirs of the kingdom
      shall answer his call;
  and all things cry 'Glory!' to God all in all.

276
Josiah Conder

1 The Lord is king! Lift up your voice,
  O earth, and all you heavens, rejoice!
  From world to world the song shall ring:
  'The Lord omnipotent is king!'

2 The Lord is king! Who then shall dare
  resist his will, distrust his care
  or quarrel with his wise decrees,
  or doubt his royal promises?

3 The Lord is king! Child of the dust,
  the judge of all the earth is just;
  holy and true are all his ways –
  let every creature sing his praise!

4 God reigns! He reigns with glory crowned:
  let Christians make a joyful sound!
  And Christ is seated at his side:
  the man of love, the crucified.

5 Come, make your needs, your burdens
      known:
  he will present them at the throne;
  and angel hosts are waiting there
  his messages of love to bear.

6 One Lord one kingdom all secures:
  he reigns, and life and death are yours;
  through earth and heaven one song shall ring:
  'The Lord omnipotent is king!'

277
From Psalm 119
© Timothy Dudley-Smith

1 The will of God to mark my way,
      the word of God for light;
  eternal justice to obey
      in everlasting right.

2 Your eyes of mercy keep me still,
      your gracious love be mine;
  so work in me your perfect will
      and cause your face to shine.

3 With ordered step secure and strong,
      from sin's oppression freed,
  redeemed from every kind of wrong
      in thought and word and deed –

4 So set my heart to love your word
      and every promise prove,
  to walk with truth before the Lord
      in righteousness and love.

278
From Psalm 23
© Christopher Idle / Jubilate Hymns

1 The Lord my shepherd rules my life
  and gives me all I need;
  he leads me by refreshing streams,
  in pastures green I feed.

2 The Lord revives my failing strength,
  he makes my joy complete;
  and in right paths, for his name's sake,
  he guides my faltering feet.

3 Though in a valley dark as death,
  no evil makes me fear;
  your shepherd's staff protects my way,
  for you are with me there.

4 While all my enemies look on
  you spread a royal feast;
  you fill my cup, anoint my head,
  and treat me as your guest.

5 Your goodness and your gracious love
  pursue me all my days;
  your house, O Lord, shall be my home –
  your name, my endless praise.

6 To Father, Son and Spirit, praise!
  to God, whom we adore,
  be worship, glory, power and love,
  both now and evermore!

279
From Psalm 23
William Whittingham and others

1 The Lord's my shepherd: I'll not want;
  he makes me down to lie
  in pastures green: he leadeth me
  the quiet waters by.

2 My soul he doth restore again,
  and me to walk doth make
  within the paths of righteousness,
  e'en for his own name's sake.

3 Yea, though I walk through death's dark vale,
  yet will I fear no ill;
  for thou art with me, and thy rod
  and staff me comfort still.

4. My table thou hast furnishèd
in presence of my foes;
my head with oil thou dost anoint
and my cup overflows.

5 Goodness and mercy all my life
shall surely follow me;
and in God's house for evermore
my dwelling-place shall be.

280 © Basil Bridge

1 The Son of God proclaim!
the Lord of time and space,
the God who bade the light break forth
now shines in Jesus' face.

2 He, God's creative Word,
the church's Lord and head,
here bids us gather as his friends
and share his wine and bread.

3 The Lord of life and death
with wondering praise we sing;
we break the bread at his command
and name him God and king.

4 We take this cup in hope,
for he who gladly bore
the shameful cross, is risen again
and reigns for evermore.

281 From the Latin
Francis Pott
© in this version Jubilate Hymns

1 The strife is past, the battle done;
now is the victor's triumph won –
O let the song of praise be sung,
Alleluia!

2 Death's mightiest powers
have done their worst;
and Jesus has his foes dispersed –
let shouts of praise and joy outburst,
Alleluia!

3 On the third day he rose again,
glorious in majesty to reign –
sing out with joy the glad refrain,
Alleluia!

4 Lord over death, our wounded king,
save us fron Satan's deadly sting
that we may live for you and sing,
Alleluia!

282 Graham Kendrick
© 1989 Make Way Music

1 The trumpets sound, the angels sing,
the feast is ready to begin;
the gates of heaven are open wide,
and Jesus welcomes you inside.

2 Tables are laden with good things:
O taste the peace and joy he brings!
He'll fill your heart with love divine,
he'll turn your water into wine.
Sing with thankfulness
songs of pure delight,
come and revel in heaven's love and light;
take your place at the table of the King –
the feast is ready to begin,
the feast is ready to begin.

3 The hungry heart he satisfies,
offers the poor his paradise.
Now hear all heaven and earth applaud
the amazing goodness of the Lord!
Sing with thankfulness . . .
Sing with thankfulness . . .

283 © Christopher Idle / Jubilate Hymns

1 The victory of our God is won
and all creation sings!
Four living creatures round the throne
acclaim the King of kings;
the elders bring their crowns to him
in worship day and night
while cherubim and seraphim
sing praise in burning light.

2 Then all believers in the Lord
combine in perfect praise:
the patriarchs who know their God,
with saints of ancient days;
the twelve apostles of the Lamb,
the prophets in their place,
the white-robed martyrs praise his name
and glory in his grace.

3 The Christians of these latter years
shall not be missing there:
the pastors and the pioneers
who wrestled with despair;
the churches where ten thousand pray,
the groups of two or three –
the angels hear them sing that day
how Jesus set them free.

4 All glory to the Lamb who died
and rescued us by blood,
the Saviour who was crucified
to bring the world to God!
Let all who witness to his word
from every tribe and tongue
sing 'Holy, holy, holy, Lord'
in everlasting song.

284 Cecil Alexander

1 There is a green hill far away
outside a city wall,
where our dear Lord was crucified,
who died to save us all.

2 We may not know, we cannot tell
what pains he had to bear,
but we believe it was for us
he hung and suffered there.

3 He died that we might be forgiven,
he died to make us good;
that we might go at last to heaven,
saved by his precious blood.

4 There was no other good enough
to pay the price of sin;
he, only, could unlock the gate
of heaven – and let us in.

5 Lord Jesus, dearly you have loved;
and we must love you too,
and trust in your redeeming blood
and learn to follow you.

285 Melody Green
© 1982 Birdwing Music / Cherry Lane Music Pub. Co.

1 There is a Redeemer,
Jesus, God's own Son,
precious Lamb of God, Messiah,
holy One.
Thank you, O my Father,
for giving us your Son,
and leaving your Spirit
till the work on earth is done.

2 Jesus, my Redeemer,
name above all names,
precious Son of God, Messiah,
Lamb for sinners slain:
Thank you . . .

3 When I stand in glory
I will see his face,
and there I'll serve my king for ever
in that holy place.
Thank you . . .

286 From Psalm 139
Brian Foley © 1971 Faber Music Ltd

1 There is no moment of my life,
no place where I may go,
no action which God does not see,
no thought he does not know.

2 Before I speak, my words are known,
and all that I decide.
To come or go: God knows my choice,
and makes himself my guide.

3 If I should close my eyes to him,
he comes to give me sight;
if I should go where all is dark,
he makes my darkness light.

4 He knew my days before all days,
before I came to be;
he keeps me, loves me, in my ways –
no lover such as he.

287 From 1 Corinthians 15
© Michael Saward / Jubilate Hymns

1 These are the facts as we have received them,
these are the truths
that the Christian believes,
this is the basis of all of our preaching:
Christ died for sinners,
Christ died for sinners,
Christ died for sinners,
and rose from the tomb.

2 These are the facts as we have received them:
Christ had fulfilled
what the scriptures foretold,
Adam's whole family
in death had been sleeping,
Christ through his rising,
Christ through his rising,
Christ through his rising, restores us to life.

3 These are the facts as we have received them:
we, with our saviour, have died on the cross;
now, having risen, our Jesus lives in us,
gives us his Spirit, gives us his Spirit,
gives us his Spirit, and makes us his home.

4 These are the facts as we have received them:
we shall be changed in the blink of an eye,
trumpets shall sound as we face life immortal,
this is the victory, this is the victory,
this is the victory, through Jesus our Lord.

5 These are the facts as we have received them:
these are the truths
   that the Christian believes,
this is the basis of all of our preaching:
Christ died for sinners,
   Christ died for sinners,
Christ died for sinners,
   and rose from the tomb.

288
From Psalm 112
© Michael Saward / Jubilate Hymns

1 They who stand in awe of God are happy,
   Hallelujah,
they whose joy is in his word are happy;
   hallelujah,
they are upright, they are just,
powerful heirs will follow them,
wealth and riches shall be theirs – sing glory!
   hallelujah!

2 In the darkness, they remain bright-shining –
   Hallelujah,
generous, merciful, and just, bright-shining;
   hallelujah,
honest in their business life,
known for their integrity,
steadfast, they will be renowned – sing glory,
   hallelujah!

3 Trouble cannot frighten them, trust God,
   Hallelujah,
they can conquer every fear, they trust God;
   hallelujah,
freely to the poor they give,
theirs the justice that is sure,
honour is their true reward – sing glory!
   hallelujah!

289
Graham Kendrick
© 1988 Make Way Music

1 This Child, secretly comes in the night:
oh this Child, hiding a heavenly light,
oh this Child, coming to us like a stranger,
this heavenly Child.
   This Child, heaven come down now
   to be with us here;
   heavenly love and mercy appear:
   softly in awe and wonder come near
   to this heavenly Child.

2 This Child, rising on us like the sun:
oh this Child, given to light everyone,
oh this Child, guiding our feet on the pathway
to peace on earth.
   This Child, heaven come down . . .

3 This Child, raising the humble and poor:
oh this Child, making the proud ones to fall;
oh this Child, filling the hungry
   with good things,
this heavenly Child.
   This Child, heaven come down . . .
   This Child, heaven come down . . .

290
From Psalm 24
© Christopher Idle / Jubilate Hymns

1 This earth belongs to God,
the world, its wealth, and all its people;
he formed the waters wide
and fashioned every sea and shore.
  A Who may go up the hill of the Lord
   and stand in the place of holiness?
  B Only the one whose heart is pure,
   whose hands and lips are clean.

2 Lift high your heads, you gates,
rise up, you everlasting doors, as
here now the king of glory
enters into full command.
  A Who is the king, this king of glory,
   where is the throne he comes to claim?
  B Christ is the king, the Lord of glory,
   fresh from his victory.

3 Lift high your heads, you gates,
and fling wide open the ancient doors, for
here comes the king of glory
taking universal power.
  A Who is the king, this king of glory,
   what is the power by which he reigns?
  B Christ is the king, his cross his glory,
   and by love he rules.

4 All glory be to God
the Father, Son and Holy Spirit;
from ages past it was,
is now, and evermore shall be.

The congregation may divide at A (e.g. Men)
and B (e.g. Women)

291
Isaac Watts

1 This is the day the Lord has made,
he calls the hours his own:
let heaven rejoice, let earth be glad,
and praise surround the throne!

2 Today he rose and left the dead,
and Satan's empire fell;
today the saints his triumphs spread,
and all his wonders tell.

3 Hosanna to the anointed king,
to David's holy Son!
Help us, O Lord; descend and bring
salvation from your throne.

4 Blessed be the Lord, who freely came
to save our sinful race:
he comes, in God the Father's name,
with words of truth and grace.

5 Hosanna in the highest strains
the church on earth can raise!
The highest heaven in which he reigns
shall give him nobler praise.

292 From Psalm 34
Nahum Tate and Nicholas Brady
© in this version Jubilate Hymns

1 Through all the changing scenes of life,
in trouble and in joy,
the praises of my God shall still
my heart and tongue employ.

2 O magnify the Lord with me,
with me exalt his name!
When in distress, to him I called –
he to my rescue came.

3 The hosts of God encamp around
the dwellings of the just;
his saving help he gives to all
who in his mercy trust.

4 O taste his goodness, prove his love!
Experience will decide
how blessed they are, and only they,
who in his truth confide.

5 Fear him, you saints, and you will then
have nothing else to fear;
his service shall be your delight,
your needs shall be his care.

6 To Father, Son and Spirit, praise!
To God whom we adore
be worship, glory, power and love,
both now and evermore!

293 Frances van Alstyne

1 To God be the glory!
Great things he has done:
so loved he the world that he gave us his Son
who yielded his life an atonement for sin,
and opened the life-gate that all may go in.

Praise the Lord, praise the Lord;
let the earth hear his voice!
Praise the Lord, praise the Lord;
let the people rejoice!
O come to the Father
through Jesus the Son
and give him the glory –
great things he has done.

2 O perfect redemption, the purchase of blood!
To every believer the promise of God:
the vilest offender who truly believes,
that moment from Jesus a pardon receives.
Praise the Lord . . .

3 Great things he has taught us,
great things he has done,
and great our rejoicing through Jesus the Son:
but purer and higher and greater will be
our wonder, our gladness, when Jesus we see!
Praise the Lord . . .

294 James Seddon
© Mrs M Seddon / Jubilate Hymns

1 To him we come –
Jesus Christ our Lord,
God's own living Word,
his dear Son:
in him there is no east or west,
in him all nations shall be blessed;
to all he offers peace and rest –
loving Lord!

2 In him we live –
Christ our strength and stay,
life and truth and way,
friend divine:
his power can break the chains of sin,
still all life's storms without, within,
help us the daily fight to win –
living Lord!

3 For him we go –
soldiers of the cross,
counting all things loss
him to know;
going to every land and race,
preaching to all redeeming grace,
building his church in every place –
conquering Lord!

4 With him we serve –
his the work we share
with saints everywhere,
near and far;
one in the task which faith requires,
one in the zeal which never tires,
one in the hope his love inspires –
coming Lord!

5 Onward we go –
faithful, bold, and true,
called his will to do
day by day
till, at the last, with joy we'll see
Jesus, in glorious majesty;
live with him through eternity –
    reigning Lord!

2 We believe he sends his Spirit
on his church with gifts of power;
God, his word of truth affirming,
sends us to the nations now.
He will come again in glory,
judge the living and the dead:
every knee shall bow before him,
then must every tongue confess.
    Jesus, Lord of all . . .

    Name above all names!

295 © David Mowbray / Jubilate Hymns

1 We believe in God Almighty,
maker of the earth and sky;
all we see and all that's hidden
is his work unceasingly:
God our Father's loving kindness
with us till the day we die –
    evermore and evermore.

2 We believe in Christ the Saviour,
Son of God and Son of Man;
born of Mary, preaching, healing,
crucified, yet risen again:
he ascended to the Father
there in glory long to reign –
    evermore and evermore.

3 We believe in God the Spirit,
present in our lives today;
speaking through the prophet's writings,
guiding travellers on their way:
to our hearts he brings forgiveness
and the hope of endless joy –
    evermore and evermore.

297 From *The Alternative Service Book 1980* © 1980 The Central Board of Finance of the Church of England

1 A We break this bread
        to share in the body of Christ:
   B We break this bread
        to share in the body of Christ.
   ALL Though we are many, we are one body,
        because we all share,
        we all share in one bread.

        Though we are many . . .

2 A We drink this cup to share in the body
        of Christ:
   B We drink this cup to share in the body
        of Christ.
        Though we are many . . .
        Though we are many . . .

The congregation may divide at A and B

296 Graham Kendrick © 1986 Thankyou Music

1 We believe in God the Father,
maker of the universe,
and in Christ his Son our saviour,
come to us by virgin birth.
We believe he died to save us,
bore our sins, was crucified;
then from death he rose victorious,
ascended to the Father's side.
    Jesus, Lord of all, Lord of all;
    Jesus, Lord of all, Lord of all;
    Jesus, Lord of all, Lord of all;
    Jesus, Lord of all, Lord of all;
    name above all names,
    name above all names!

298 © Timothy Dudley-Smith

1 We come as guests invited
when Jesus bids us dine,
his friends on earth united
to share the bread and wine;
the bread of life is broken,
the wine is freely poured
for us, in solemn token
of Christ our dying Lord.

2 We eat and drink, receiving
from Christ the grace we need,
and in our hearts believing
on him by faith we feed;
with wonder and thanksgiving
for love that knows no end,
we find in Jesus living
our ever-present friend.

3 One bread is ours for sharing,
one single fruitful vine,
our fellowship declaring
renewed in bread and wine –
renewed, sustained and given
by token, sign and word,
the pledge and seal of heaven,
the love of Christ our Lord.

299   © Michael Perry / Jubilate Hymns

1 We give God thanks for those who knew
the touch of Jesus' healing love;
they trusted him to make them whole,
to give them peace, their guilt remove.

2 We offer prayer for all who go
relying on his grace and power,
to help the anxious and the ill,
to heal their wounds, their lives restore.

3 We dedicate our skills and time
to those who suffer where we live,
to bring such comfort as we can
to meet their need, their pain relieve.

4 So Jesus' touch of healing grace
lives on within our willing care;
by thought and prayer and gifts we prove
his mercy still, his love we share.

300   © Edward Burns

1 We have a gospel to proclaim,
good news for all throughout the earth;
the gospel of a saviour's name:
we sing his glory, tell his worth.

2 Tell of his birth at Bethlehem,
not in a royal house or hall
but in a stable dark and dim:
the Word made flesh, a light for all.

3 Tell of his death at Calvary,
hated by those he came to save;
in lonely suffering on the cross
for all he loved, his life he gave.

4 Tell of that glorious Easter morn:
empty the tomb, for he was free!
He broke the power of death and hell
that we might share his victory.

5 Tell of his reign at God's right hand,
by all creation glorified;
he sends his Spirit on his church
to live for him, the Lamb who died.

6 Now we rejoice to name him king:
Jesus is Lord of all the earth;
this gospel-message we proclaim:
we sing his glory, tell his worth.

301   William Bullock and Henry Baker
© in this version Jubilate Hymns

1 We love the place, O God,
in which your honour dwells:
the joy of your abode,
all earthly joy excels.

2 We love the house of prayer:
for where Christ's people meet,
our risen Lord is there
to make our joy complete.

3 We love the word of life,
the word that tells of peace,
of comfort in the strife
and joys that never cease.

4 We love the cleansing sign
of life through Christ our Lord,
where with the name divine
we seal the child of God.

5 We love the holy feast
where, nourished with this food,
by faith we feed on Christ,
his body and his blood.

6 We love to sing below
of mercies freely given,
but O, we long to know
the triumph-song of heaven.

7 Lord Jesus, give us grace
on earth to love you more,
in heaven to see your face
and with your saints adore.

302   After Matthias Claudius
Jane Campbell

1 We plough the fields, and scatter
the good seed on the land;
but it is fed and watered
by God's almighty hand:
he sends the snow in winter,
the warmth to swell the grain;
the breezes and the sunshine
and soft refreshing rain.
    All good gifts around us
    are sent from heaven above:
    then thank the Lord, O thank the Lord
    for all his love.

2 He only is the maker
of all things near and far;
he paints the wayside flower,
he lights the evening star:
the winds and waves obey him,
by him the birds are fed;
much more, to us his children
he gives our daily bread.
   All good gifts . . .

3 We thank you, then, our Father,
for all things bright and good;
the seed-time and the harvest,
our life, our health, our food:
accept the gifts we offer
for all your love imparts;
and that which you most welcome
our humble, thankful hearts!
   All good gifts . . .

303 Edith Cherry
© in this version Jubilate Hymns

1 We trust in you, our shield and our defender;
we do not fight alone against the foe:
strong in your strength,
   safe in your keeping tender,
we trust in you, and in your name we go.
   Strong in your strength . . .

2 We trust in you, O Captain of salvation!
in your dear name, all other names above:
Jesus our righteousness, our sure foundation,
our prince of glory and our king of love.
   Jesus our righteousness . . .

3 We go in faith,
   our own great weakness feeling,
and needing more each day
   your grace to know;
yet from our hearts a song of triumph pealing,
'We trust in you, and in your name we go.'
   Yet from our hearts . . .

4 We trust in you, our shield and our defender:
yours is the battle – yours shall be the praise!
When passing through the gates
   of dazzling splendour,
victors, we rest in you through endless days.
   When passing through . . .

304 © Michael Baughen / Jubilate Hymns

1 We worship God in harmony
with hearts in full accord;
we share one Spirit, hope and faith,
one Father and one Lord:

In Jesus Christ our Lord and king,
in Jesus Christ our Lord,
the Spirit makes us all as one
in Jesus Christ our Lord.

2 We're children now of God by grace –
our new life has begun,
where male and female, Greek and Jew,
both bound and free are one.
   In Jesus Christ . . .

3 We live as those whom Christ has called
to love with Christ-like mind
that looks towards each other's needs,
forbearing, patient, kind.
   In Jesus Christ . . .

4 One day we'll see him face to face,
to him we'll bow the knee;
we'll never say goodbye again –
the best is yet to be!
   In Jesus Christ . . .

305 Joseph Scrivens

1 What a friend we have in Jesus
   all our sins and griefs to bear;
what a privilege to carry
   everything to God in prayer!
O what peace we often forfeit,
   O what needless pain we bear,
all because we do not carry
   everything to God in prayer.

2 Have we trials and temptations
   is there trouble anywhere?
We should never be discouraged:
   take it to the Lord in prayer.
Can we find a friend so faithful
   who will all our sorrows share?
Jesus knows our every weakness –
   take it to the Lord in prayer.

3 Are we weak and heavy-laden,
   burdened with a load of care?
Jesus is our mighty saviour;
   he will listen to our prayer.
Do your friends despise, forsake you?
   Take it to the Lord in prayer:
in his arms he will enfold you
   and his love will shield you there.

306 Joseph Addison
© in this version Jubilate Hymns

1 When all your mercies, O my God,
my thankful soul surveys,
uplifted by the view, I'm lost
in wonder, love and praise.

2 Unnumbered blessings to my soul
   your tender care bestowed
   before my infant heart perceived
   from whom these blessings flowed.

3 Ten thousand thousand precious gifts
   my daily thanks employ;
   nor is the least a thankful heart
   that takes those gifts with joy.

4 In health and sickness, joy and pain,
   your goodness I'll pursue;
   and after death, in distant worlds,
   the glorious theme renew.

5 Throughout eternity, O Lord,
   a joyful song I'll raise;
   but all eternity's too short
   to utter all your praise!

307 Isaac Watts

1 When I survey the wondrous cross
   on which the prince of glory died,
   my richest gain I count as loss,
   and pour contempt on all my pride.

2 Forbid it, Lord, that I should boast
   save in the cross of Christ my God:
   the very things that charm me most –
   I sacrifice them to his blood.

3 See from his head, his hands, his feet,
   sorrow and love flow mingled down:
   when did such love and sorrow meet,
   or thorns compose so rich a crown?

4 Were the whole realm of nature mine,
   that were an offering far too small;
   love so amazing, so divine,
   demands my soul, my life, my all!

308 From Isaiah 35
© Christopher Idle / Jubilate Hymns

1 When the king shall come again
      all his power revealing,
   splendour shall announce his reign,
      life and joy and healing:
   earth no longer in decay,
      hope no more frustrated;
   this is God's redemption day
      longingly awaited.

2 In the desert trees take root
      fresh from his creation;
   plants and flowers and sweetest fruit
      join the celebration:
   rivers spring up from the earth,
      barren lands adorning;
   valleys, this is your new birth,
      mountains, greet the morning!

3 Strengthen feeble hands and knees,
      fainting hearts be cheerful!
   God who comes for such as these
      seeks and saves the fearful:
   now the deaf can hear the dumb
      sing away their weeping;
   blind eyes see the injured come
      walking, running, leaping.

4 There God's highway shall be seen
      where no roaring lion,
   nothing evil or unclean
      walks the road to Zion:
   ransomed people homeward bound
      all your praises voicing,
   see your Lord with glory crowned,
      share in his rejoicing!

309 From John 1
© Michael Saward / Jubilate Hymns

1 When things began to happen,
      before the birth of time,
   the Word was with the Father
      and shared his holy name:
   without him there was nothing –
      all life derives from him;
   his light shines in the darkness –
      an unextinguished beam.

2 He came to his creation,
      the work of his own hand;
   he entered his own country
      but they would not respond:
   yet some gave their allegiance
      of life and heart and mind;
   thus they became his subjects
      and he became their friend.

3 Conceived by heaven's mercy,
      this was no human birth;
   for they are God's own children
      redeemed from sin and death:
   and they beheld his glory,
      so full of grace and truth;
   in Christ, God's Son, our saviour,
      whom we adore by faith.

310

1 When you prayed beneath the trees,
　　it was for me, O Lord;
　when you cried upon your knees,
　　how could it be, O Lord?
　　　When in blood and sweat and tears
　you dismissed your final fears,
　when you faced the soldiers' spears,
　　you stood for me, O Lord.

2 When their triumph looked complete,
　　it was for me, O Lord,
　when it seemed like your defeat,
　　they could not see, O Lord!
　　　When you faced the mob alone
　you were silent as a stone,
　and a tree became your throne;
　　you came for me, O Lord.

3 When you stumbled up the road,
　　you walked for me, O Lord,
　when you took your deadly load,
　　that heavy tree, O Lord;
　　　When they lifted you on high,
　and they nailed you up to die,
　and when darkness filled the sky,
　　it was for me, O Lord.

4 When you spoke with kingly power,
　　it was for me, O Lord,
　in that dread and destined hour,
　　you made me free, O Lord;
　　　earth and heaven heard you shout,
　death and hell were put to rout,
　for the grave could not hold out;
　　you are for me, O Lord.

311

Nahum Tate

1 While shepherds watched their flocks
　　by night
　all seated on the ground,
　the angel of the Lord came down
　and glory shone around.

2 'Fear not,' said he – for mighty dread
　had seized their troubled mind –
　'Good news of greatest joy I bring
　to you and all mankind.

3 'To you in Bethlehem this day
　is born of David's line
　a saviour, who is Christ the Lord.
　And this shall be the sign:

4 'The heavenly babe you there shall find
　to human view displayed,
　all simply wrapped in swaddling clothes
　and in a manger laid.'

5 Thus spoke the seraph, and forthwith
　appeared a shining throng
　of angels praising God, who thus
　addressed their joyful song:

6 'All glory be to God on high,
　and to the earth be peace!
　Goodwill henceforth from highest heaven
　begin and never cease.'

312

from Psalms 12 and 82
Graham Kendrick
© 1988 Make Way Music

1 Who can sound the depths of sorrow
　in the Father heart of God,
　for the children we've rejected,
　for the lives so deeply scarred?
　And each light that we've extinguished
　has brought darkness to our land:
　　upon our nation, upon our nation
　　have mercy Lord!

2 We have scorned the truth you gave us,
　we have bowed to other lords,
　we have sacrificed the children
　on the altars of our gods.
　O let truth again shine on us,
　let your holy fear descend:
　　upon our nation, upon our nation
　　have mercy Lord!

3 A
Who can stand before your anger;
　who can face your piercing eyes?
　For you love the weak and helpless,
　and you hear the victims' cries.
ALL
Yes, you are a God of justice,
　and your judgement surely comes:
　　upon our nation, upon our nation
　　have mercy Lord!

4 B
Who will stand against the violence?
　Who will comfort those who mourn?
　In an age of cruel rejection,
　who will build for love a home?
ALL
Come and shake us into action,
　come and melt our hearts of stone:
　　upon your people, upon your people,
　　have mercy Lord!

5   Who can sound the depths of mercy
     in the Father heart of God?
     For there is a Man of sorrows
     who for sinners shed his blood.
     He can heal the wounds of nations,
     he can wash the guilty clean:
        because of Jesus, because of Jesus
        have mercy Lord!

The congregation may divide at A and B

313   Richard Baxter
© in this version Jubilate Hymns

1   You holy angels bright
     who wait at God's right hand,
     or through the realms of light
     fly at your Lord's command:
        assist our song,
        or else the theme
        too high will seem
        for mortal tongue.

2   You faithful souls at rest,
     who ran this earthly race,
     and now from sin released
     behold the Saviour's face:
        his praises sound
        and all unite
        in sweet delight
        to see him crowned.

3   You saints who serve below,
     adore your heavenly King,
     and as you onward go
     your joyful anthems sing:
        take what he gives
        and praise him still
        through good and ill,
        who ever lives.

4   So take, my soul, your part;
     triumph in God above,
     and with a well-tuned heart
     sing out your songs of love:
        with joy proclaim
        through all your days
        in ceaseless praise
        his glorious name!

314   Charles Wesley

1   You servants of God, your master proclaim,
     and publish abroad his wonderful name;
     the name all-victorious of Jesus extol –
     his kingdom is glorious, and rules over all.

2   God rules in the height, almighty to save –
     though hid from our sight,
        his presence we have;
     the great congregation his triumph shall sing,
     ascribing salvation to Jesus our king.

3   'Salvation to God who sits on the throne!'
     let all cry aloud, and honour the Son:
     the praises of Jesus the angels proclaim,
     fall down on their faces
        and worship the Lamb.

4   Then let us adore and give him his right:
     all glory and power, all wisdom and might,
     all honour and blessing – with angels above –
     and thanks never ceasing, and infinite love.

315   Edward Plumptre

1   Your hand, O God, has guided
     your flock, from age to age;
     your faithfulness is written
     on history's every page.
     They knew your perfect goodness,
     whose deeds we now record;
     and both to this bear witness:
        One church, one faith, one Lord.

2   Your heralds brought the gospel
     to greatest as to least;
     they summoned us to hasten
     and share the great king's feast.
     And this was all their teaching
     in every deed and word:
     to all alike proclaiming
        one church, one faith, one Lord.

3   Through many days of darkness,
     through many scenes of strife,
     the faithful few fought bravely
     to guard the nation's life.
     Their gospel of redemption –
     sin pardoned, hope restored –
     was all in this enfolded:
        One church, one faith, one Lord.

4   And we, shall we be faithless?
     Shall hearts fail, hands hang down?
     Shall we evade the conflict
     and throw away the crown?
     Not so! In God's deep counsels
     some better thing is stored;
     we will maintain, unflinching,
        one church, one faith, one Lord.

5   Your mercy will not fail us
    nor leave your work undone;
    with your right hand to help us,
    the victory shall be won.
    And then by earth and heaven
    your name shall be adored;
    and this shall be their anthem:
      One church, one faith, one Lord.

316
After Edmund Budry
Richard Hoyle
© in this version Jubilate Hymns

1   Yours be the glory! risen, conquering Son;
    endless is the victory over death you won;
    angels robed in splendour
      rolled the stone away,
    kept the folded grave clothes
      where your body lay:
      Yours be the glory! risen, conquering Son:
      endless is the victory over death you won.

2   See! Jesus meets us, risen from the tomb,
    lovingly he greets us, scatters fear and gloom;
    let the church
      with gladness hymns of triumph sing!
    for her Lord is living, death has lost it's sting:
      Yours be the glory . . .

3   No more we doubt you, glorious prince of life:
    what is life without you? aid us in our strife;
    make us more than conquerors
      through your deathless love,
    bring us safe through Jordan
      to your home above:
      Yours be the glory . . .

Traditional Version

1   Thine be the glory, risen, conquering Son:
    endless is the victory
      thou o'er death hast won!
    Angels in bright raiment
      rolled the stone away,
    kept the folded grave-clothes
      where thy body lay:
      Thine be the glory risen, conquering Son:
      endless is the victory
      thou o'er death hast won!

2   Lo, Jesus meets us, risen from the tomb;
    lovingly he greets us, scatters fear and gloom.
    Let the church with gladness
      hymns of triumph sing,
    for her Lord now liveth,
      death hath lost its sting.
      Thine be the glory . . .

3   No more we doubt thee,
      glorious prince of life:
    what is life without thee? Aid us in our strife;
    make us more than conquerors
      through thy deathless love;
    bring us safe through Jordan
      to thy home above.
      Thine be the glory . . .

Bible prayers for worship

INVITATION
From Psalm 98

Sing to the Lord, all the world,
for the Lord is a mighty God.

Sing a new song to the Lord,
for he has done marvellous things.

Proclaim his glory among the nations,
and shout for joy to the Lord our king.

GREETING
From Romans 1 etc.

Grace and peace to you from God our
Father and from the Lord Jesus Christ.
Amen.

APPROACH
From Psalm 118

Lord,
this is the day you made;
we rejoice and are glad in it:
help us and bless us
as we come into your presence –
we praise you and exalt you,
we celebrate and thank you;
for you are our God
and your love endures for ever.

CONFESSION
From Psalm 51

**Lord God, be gracious to us
because of your great love for us;
in your great mercy
wash away our sins –
for we are weighed down by them,
and we know we have failed;
we have offended against you
and done evil in your sight:
create in us a pure heart,
put a loyal spirit in us,
and give us again the joy
that comes from your salvation.
Amen.**

ASSURANCE OF GOD'S MERCY
From Psalm 103

The love of God for those who seek him is
as great as the heavens are high above the
earth: as far as the east is from the west he
removes our sins from us, and he will
remember them no more.

EXHORTATION
From Revelation 19

Let us rejoice and be glad,
and give God the glory.

BEFORE READING
From 2 Samuel 22

You are our lamp, O Lord;
you turn our darkness into light.

AFTER READING
From Mark 4

Those who have a mind to hear,
let them hear!

CREED
From 1 Corinthians 8 and 12

We believe in one God and Father;
from him all things come.

We believe in one Lord Jesus Christ;
through him we come to God.

We believe in one Holy Spirit;
in him we are baptised into one body.

**We believe and trust in one God,
Father, Son and Holy Spirit.**

THE LORD'S PRAYER
From Matthew 6 and Luke 11

**Our Father in heaven,
hallowed be your name,
your kingdom come,
your will be done,
on earth as in heaven.
Give us today our daily bread.
Forgive us our sins
as we forgive those who sin against us.
Lead us not into temptation
but deliver us from evil.**

**For the kingdom, the power,
and the glory are yours,
now and for ever. Amen.**

BEFORE PRAYER
From Hebrews 4

Let us approach God's throne with
confidence:
**we shall receive mercy,
and find grace to help us.**

INTERCESSION
From Hebrews 4 etc.

Let us approach God's throne with
confidence:
**we shall receive mercy,
and find grace to help
in time of need.**

Upon . . . have mercy, Lord;
we entrust them to your care.

In . . . Lord, may peace and justice rule:
let your love prevail.

To God be glory in the Church and in
Christ Jesus:
for ever and ever. Amen.

FOR OTHERS: IN TROUBLE
From Psalm 31

Be merciful, Lord,
to all those in trouble:
those who are ill or weary,
those who are deep in sorrow,
those whose life is ebbing away,
those who are without friends,
those who are forgotten by the world:
Lord, we entrust them to your care;
in Jesus' name. **Amen.**

FOR OURSELVES
From Isaiah 33

Lord, be gracious to us,
for we long for you:
be our strength every day,
our salvation in time of trouble,
our greatest treasure in life,
and our reward in heaven;
through Jesus our redeemer. **Amen.**

THANKSGIVING
From Isaiah 63

Our God,
we thank you for all your kindness,
and we praise you
for all the good things
you have done for us:
you are our saviour –
in our distress
you too were distressed,
in your love and mercy you redeemed us;
through Jesus Christ our Lord. **Amen.**

THE GRACE
From 1 Corinthians 13

The grace of our Lord Jesus Christ,
and the love of God,
and the fellowship of the Holy Spirit,
be with us all evermore. **Amen.**

DOXOLOGY
From Romans 16

Glory to God
who alone is all-wise;
through Jesus Christ, for ever! **Amen.**

BLESSING
From Numbers 6

The Lord bless us and keep us, the Lord
make his face to shine upon us, the Lord be
kind and gracious to us, the Lord look upon
us with favour, and give us peace. **Amen.**

Index of First Lines

Italics indicate former first lines and other names by which the hymns are known